Readin

Reading Oprah

How Oprah's Book Club Changed the Way America Reads

Cecilia Konchar Farr

State University of New York Press

Published by
State University of New York Press, Albany

© 2005 State University of New York
Cover photo courtesy of Landov LLC

Printed in the United States of America

For information, address State University of New York Press,
90 State Street, Suite 700, Albany, NY 12207

Production by Kelli Williams
Marketing by Fran Keneston

Libray of Congress Cataloging-in-Publication Data

Farr, Cecilia Konchar, 1958-
    Reading Oprah: How Oprah's Book Club Changed the Way America Reads /
Cecilia Konchar Farr.
        p. cm.
    Includes bibliographical references (p.) and index.
    ISBN 0-7914-6257-9 (alk. paper) —ISBN 0-7914-6258-7 (pbk. : alk. paper)
        1. American fiction—20th century—History and criticism—Theory, etc.
    2. Book clubs (Discussion groups)—United States—History—20th century.
    3. Fiction—Appreciation—United States—History—20th century. 4. Books and
    reading—United States—History—2oth century. 5. Winfrey, Oprah—Influence.
    I. Title.

PS379.F37 2004
813'.5409—dc22
                                                                    2003070442

10 9 8 7 6 5 4 3 2 1

For Fossil, who loved ideas, straight talk,
a good argument, and me.

Contents

Foreword: Elizabeth Long   ix

Acknowledgments   xiii

Introduction: Oprah's Reading Revolution   1

Chapter One: Reading Oprah   7

   The Book Club Begins   10

   To Enlighten and Entertain   12

   The Oprah Effect   14

   The Oprah Writers   18

   Oprah's Choices   20

   What Women Want   22

Chapter Two: Oprah Reading   29

   The Talking Book   30

   The Way West   32

   The Middlebrow Novel   34

   The Middlebrow Book Club   38

   Reading Lessons   41

      Deep End of the Ocean   41

      Song of Solomon   43

   Talk Reading   45

      Paradise   45

      Song of Solomon   49

Chapter Three: Readers Talking   53

  Group Reading   55
  The Talking Life   59
  Oprahfication   60
    Black and Blue   61
    Open House   63
  Oprah's American Story   64
  The Elegant Balance   67
    The Bluest Eye   67

Chapter Four: Talking Readers   75

  The Corrections   75
  McLiterature   77
  Claiming Cultural Capital   81
  Learning to Read   83
  The List   86
  Reading for Class   88
  Shifting Standards   92
  Anticipatory Marketing   94

Conclusion: The Triumph of Cultural Democracy   99

  Cultural Democracy   101
    White Oleander   105

Appendices   109

Notes   121

Works Cited   149

Index   157

Foreword

As Cecilia Konchar Farr notes early on in her book, it is amazing that academics have paid so little attention to Oprah Winfrey's Book Club. Here is a cultural phenomenon of amazing vitality (one that refused to die even when its author abandoned it!) and unprecedented economic reach in the literary world. Oprah's Book Club selections skyrocketed to the top of the bestseller list, generating hundreds of thousands of dollars for their publishers, giving fiction a new cultural clout, and bringing stardom to even obscure literary novelists. Here, too, is a cultural experiment in reading on a grand scale: an experiment that harnessed a medium that is supposedly hostile to books in order to, in Oprah's own words, "get America reading again." The sales figures of every "O" book marked a measure of her success in this regard, as did the numerous and often touching letters and e-mails from women who had suddenly discovered—or rediscovered—the joys of reading.

So why have scholars been so slow to bring Oprah's Book Club under their analytic gaze? Farr speculates that their reluctance may be due to its origins in the suspect format of daytime TV. Yet Farr's own book indicates that there may be other reasons. Though the Book Club is a topic of great richness, it is also one that can challenge some of the deepest-held academic truisms about reading, teaching, and the nature of the novel. Because Farr takes up that challenge, her book—although written in unpretentious language with a self-consciously modest desire to explore what has made the Book Club work—is both thought provoking and extremely interesting.

For example, this is the first account of Oprah's Book Club I have read to take seriously Oprah's role as a teacher. Scholars will admit that Oprah got people excited about books, or that she mobilized audience members' identification with—and trust for—her as a person in order to engage them with books. But Farr shows, through detailed comparisons with her own work as a college teacher, that Oprah was teaching the skills, craft, and pleasures of reading. In her account, Oprah's selection of novels was itself strategic, moving back and forth between books that may have been well written but were easy for inexperienced readers to enjoy, and more dense, complex, and highly "literary" works. Contrasting the first two novels on the Book Club, *The Deep End of the Ocean* and *Song of Solomon*, Farr argues: "The pattern these first two novels set revealed Oprah's commitment 'to enlighten as well as entertain,' simultaneously to meet her readers where they were and to push them a little further. . . . This dynamic, I believe, is what took the Book Club beyond a passing media sensation . . . to a significant cultural phenomenon." Farr notes how Oprah's introductions similarly ran the gamut from effusive outpourings about some selections (telling readers how they would identify with the characters, or how much fun they would have) to coaching her audience about harder books, urging them to "stay with" them, to savor their language, to take the time and effort to reap their rewards. Similarly, Farr argues, Oprah pushed her readers to encounter books by African American authors, thus opening their sights outward, into new thematic territory, as well as "upward."

If Oprah was, as Farr claims, a teacher of reading, then what kind of reading was she teaching? Farr shows how Oprah began with the "easiest" but also most emotionally powerful level of response—the empathic, negotiated through identification. Sometimes, Farr admits, Oprah lingered at this level too long, or deployed identification in the interests of rather facile books. Yet on balance, Farr claims that Oprah demanded more from her audience. Farr details how Oprah urged attention to the author and thus the "authored" or constructed nature of the text. With the help of these authors—especially Toni Morrison, who emerges in these pages as a reading mentor of great skill—Oprah pulled the audience to consider, as well, the craft of a book's construction, its capacity for complex and multilayered meanings, and (in some

cases) the sheer beauty of its language. But, in a twist that is as interesting as it is unexpected, Farr notes that this process did not just wean
readers from an "easier" affective and empathetic reading—but also
moved in the other direction as well, teaching audience members that
an academic or formalistic reading is not enough. If, for Oprah, reading
is *more than* emotion-laden identification, it is also *more than* intellection—
but rather a hybrid process that combines both of them, and mixes in
some of Oprah's (and Farr's) own conviction that the novel can be trans-
formational, even inspirational as well.

Indeed, one of the insights I found very interesting in this book is
the notion that Oprah is not only elevating unexpected books and authors due to her personal taste or critical charisma: the "oprahfying" effect. (Though Farr does note the risks she took by selecting unknown
authors and authors of color.) In Farr's analysis, Oprah is also contest-
ing the very nature of the novel and of what it takes to give the novel an
appropriate reception. Farr develops the argument that as a genre, the
novel was originally a "middle" cultural phenomenon, though later in its
life it colonized both high culture and low. She points to the ways that
disenfranchised constituencies (women, African Americans) used the
novel to educate themselves in the nineteenth century, and to the
novel's twentieth-century role in acculturating immigrants and offering
self-improvement to those striving for entry into the middle class. If this
argument has merit, then Oprah was, as her own words claimed, spon-
soring a reading revolution as *return*. In "getting America reading again,"
she was demanding a return to the purpose, nature, and function of the
novel before it became institutionalized in English curricula. According
to Farr, Oprah rediscovered something central about the novel when
she brought to the fore novels with social justice themes, or chose novels by, for, and about women as complex individuals, and by, for, and
about people of color. Most intriguingly of all, Farr claims that novels
have always needed a talking life—a life of discourse and discussion, a
broadly democratic encounter with a wide audience. So, in the end, Farr
finds issues such as Oprah's occasional penchant for sentimental novels
or for heroines whose stories resemble her own—even the issue of commodification—less important than the question of cultural democracy.
According to this book, we must understand Oprah's most important

cultural work as broadening the audience for fiction, broadening the kinds of fiction we should value (even if the critical establishment does not), and broadening as well our idea of what constitutes an appropriate set of reading practices for novels. It is an argument that should be taken very seriously.

Elizabeth Long

Acknowledgments

This book came into being with the help of the St. Kate's students who first explored Oprah Books with me: Stephanie Duffy, Kristen Erickson, Brooke Field, Jamie Humphreys, Alisha Kessel, Ekaterina Konkava, Sally Kubo, Susan Lane, Erin McMahon, Catherine Rahadi, Jenifer Schuette, Lisa Sveen, Ker Vang, Ami Vitko, Kristine Werner, and Michelle Wigley in the summer of 1999, and Nicki Ahles, Stacy Bifulk, Jennifer Boever, Kelli Clancy, Nicole Clark, Heather Fouks, Emily Henry, Jennifer Jensen, Nanette Jensen, Gina Johnston, Kristina Kind, Raini Knaeble, Kelli Larsen, Nicole Lentsch, Emily Matakis, Lori Miskosky, Kris Olsen, Elizabeth Olson, Alissa Pavlish, Shelley Rhein, Megan Sobocinski, Amy Theis, and LeAnn Weikle in the summer of 2000.

It took shape with the help of three other groups of Oprah students who followed them and continued to ask challenging questions that directed my research and expanded my thinking. Cynthia Phimmasone, Erin McMahon, Amber Fischer, Gina Peterson, and Jenn Jacobs also deserve hearty thanks for their work as my research and teaching assistants.

Reading Oprah was nurtured by my interdisciplinary Women's Studies Writing Group: Amy Hilden, Lynne Gildensoph, Lilly Goren, Jane Carroll, and Joanne Cavallaro; and by friends and colleagues Melissa Bradshaw, Jacque James, Joannie Sackreiter, Gay Herzberg, Jeffrey Williams, Amanda Stremcha, and Jaime Harker, who read drafts or listened through them, encouraged, energized, and edited me, and by Jane Bunker and Kelli Williams, my editors at State University of New York Press. I owe thanks to several scholars who made my work possible: Elizabeth Long, who generously gave me access to early drafts of her work on women's book groups and, in conversations in the summer of 2000, affirmed that I was asking the right questions of Oprah's Book Club; Leslie-Ann Rubinkowski, Virginia Unkefer, Jane Tompkins, Stanley Fish, Annette Kolodny, Greg Clark, Gloria Cronin, and Cathy Davidson, who taught me to think and write for my life; and, always, Katherine Fishburn, my mentor and friend. This book was fostered as well by the College of St. Catherine, which granted me a sabbatical, faculty development funding, an Abigail Quigley McCarthy Center for Women Award, a Charles M. Denny Writing Prize (for which I also owe thanks to Chuck and his family), a weeklong Scholars' Retreat each summer, and a delightful, engaging atmosphere for my work.

I also want to acknowledge my Xena Book Group in Minnesota as the voice in my ear as I wrote. They are my Ya-yas and my ideal audience: Vicki Reid, Colleen Callahan, Sabina Thatcher, Diane Brown, Andrea Sorenson, Stephanie Catania, Cindy Sandberg, Susan Barker, and (in absentia) Becky Linford. Thanks to the Feminist Home Evening gang, too, for being a book group unlike any other before or since. They are always with me, pushing me, making me aim higher.

And thanks to my Utah book group for first initiating me into the joys of the talking life of books. Every novel should do so well as to claim a place with that group around the fireplace in Sam and Nancy Rushforth's cabin, with snow powdering the mountain outside as we talked long into the night. They are still among the finest men and women I know, the best readers and talkers.

Writing this book is a gift both given and received, for and from Mum and Foss, who never stop believing in me, and the house full of Konchars they nurtured, where wit and wordplay, love and laughter were never in short supply, even when other less essential things were. It is also both for and from my children, Daley and Tanner, who showed me that the hand that rocks the cradle gets stronger and does better work. Everything is possible because of them.

And most of all I acknowledge my partner, editor, and friend, Tracy. From our first heated exchange over the worldviews and relative merits of *One Flew Over the Cuckoo's Nest* and *It's a Wonderful Life* over twenty-five-years ago, we have never stopped collaborating and learning from our vast differences—middle-class Mormon boy meets steelworker's daughter. It's been a talking life ever since, a coming-together life, a wonderful life over the cuckoo's nest. Thanks Cubs.

Introduction

Oprah's Reading Revolution

> Novels are for talking about and quarrelling about and engaging in some powerful way. However that happens, at a reading group, a study group, a classroom or just some friends getting together, it's a delightful, desirable thing to do. And I think it helps. Reading is solitary, but that's not its only life. It should have a talking life, a discourse that follows.
>
> —Toni Morrison

When Oprah Winfrey announced in April 2002, to the dismay of readers and publishers, that she was ending "the Book Club as we've known it," she interrupted a project that, in just a few short years, had changed what and how Americans read.[1] Toni Morrison called it a "reading revolution."[2] And so it was, a vast reeducation of readers to embrace serious contemporary novels in a nationwide group hug. Oprah's Book Club is based on the same premise as Oprah's talk show—that novels, like sex, celebrities, and social problems, should be talked about.

I imagine the novel, like the confessional talk show guest, saying to Oprah (from one of those big, yellow chairs), "Don't get me started"—because, of course, there would be no stopping it. From its seventeenth-century origins, the novel has been a social creature, a fierce cultural critic, and a lively entertainer. Oprah pulled the reticent twentieth-century novel out of the wings and returned it to its rightful place center stage. She pushed solitary readers and alienated writers into the background and gave the novel back its social history—of Jane Austen, surrounded by family and friends in her drawing room, testing

1

her novels aloud; of Ernest Hemingway and the Lost Generation reading each other's work and talking long into the night in Paris bars and
cafés; of public readings and reading groups, college classes and books-
of-the-month. Oprah gave the novel back its talking life.[3]

Tracing how eagerly Americans embraced Oprah's "talk reading" is
easy. Here's how it worked: Every month or so for almost six years
Oprah chose a contemporary novel and and announced her choice on
TV. Then, over a million people rushed to their computers and bookstores to buy it. In the first three years of the Book Club, Oprah books
sold an average of 1.4 million copies each.[4] Every book she invited her
Book Club to read and talk about was an instant bestseller, averaging
seventeen weeks on the New York Times bestseller list. Every book. In fact,
from October 1996 through June 2002, the length of the Book Club's
first run, a week never went by without at least one Oprah book on the
national bestseller lists. Sometimes there were as many as five or six in
the weekly top fifteen. The return of the Book Club in its current format, meeting about five times a year around classic works of fiction,
promises to be nearly as successful.[5] The June 2003 selection of Steinbeck's East of Eden sent that classic careening to the heights of the bestseller lists, where, with Hillary Clinton and Harry Potter, it was one of
the summer's success stories. The new Book Club's pastel hats, T-shirts,
and bags include the apt slogan "The Biggest Book Club in the World."

Oprah achieves this kind of success, simply, by addressing the
daytime TV audience she already has, which encompasses the barely
middle class, the less educated, the ubiquitous audience member who
hasn't "read a book since high school," as well as the privileged, the college graduates, the stay-at-home soccer mom longing for intellectual
stimulation.[6] Assuming they will all enjoy serious literature, she confidently offers them solid, well-written novels and invites them to discuss
them with her. And they oblige.

When people ask why I study Oprah's Book Club, I tell them, only
half-jokingly, that as an English professor I envy Oprah's pulpit.
I choose my favorite novels and can get twenty students at a time to
read and talk with me about them. Sometimes I can convince the eight
women in my book club to go with my selections. Now and then my
kids listen to my book advice. But Oprah chooses her novels and thir-

teen million people tune in. If a million of them buy the book, let's suppose half read it. Her percentages aren't great—from thirteen million to 500,000, while I (and my grade book) can usually get about eighteen out of twenty—but her numbers are mind-boggling.

For several years I directed an interdisciplinary program at my college. As I worked with faculty and students from many departments—Biology and Sociology, Nursing, Art, and Education—I noticed over and over how we found common ground around books, how books brought us together as seekers, as curious, thinking people. As part of that program, I needed to reach out to students more generally, beyond the English department. How could I invite students to become lifelong readers when they, like that Oprah reader, hadn't picked up a book since their high school English class? How could I lead students who were already readers to challenge themselves with rich, complex, and difficult books? Then I noticed that, for many of my students, Oprah seemed to be doing just that. All right then, I decided, I'll teach a course on Oprah Books.

To prepare, I went to the usual sources of information for literary scholars.[7] I was surprised to find that no one had written yet about the influence of Oprah's Book Club—in late 1998, more than two years after it began. I tried the other learned sources, general interest journals and magazines, and other cultural commentary. There was nothing. It seemed the only people writing about Oprah's Book Club were to be found through Lexis/Nexis. They wrote for newspapers or for magazines about the entertainment or publishing industries: Oprah as a celebrity, Oprah as an entrepreneur, Oprah as star maker for struggling writers.

Even then, Oprah's influence on book sales and patterns of consumption for American book buyers was hard to ignore. The trade paperback market is a case in point. Self-help and computer instruction ruled these bestseller lists until the influence of Oprah's Book Club first registered and literary fiction started appearing there in surprising numbers. "This is the first year in decades," reported *Publishers Weekly* Executive Editor Daisy Maryles in her 1997 end-of-year book roundup, "to see so much fiction so high on the list." Of the top twelve trade paperbacks that year, five were novels—four Oprah books and a Stephen King.

Other titles in the top twelve included *Don't Sweat the Small Stuff*, *Chicken Soup for the Woman's* (Mother's, Christian) *Soul*, and *Windows 95 for Dummies*. The trend toward fiction continued in 1998, and in 1999 the popular Oprah novel *The Pilot's Wife* topped a fiction-heavy list, the first time ever the editors could remember when there were more novels than self-help books in the top twelve.[8]

We know now, a few years down the road, that the Oprah "O" on a novel's cover represents instant fame and bestseller status. We know that Oprah did what she set out to do—"to get America reading again." But what we still haven't confronted is how Oprah's grand success affects the ways Americans read and value books. What has she done to us? How (and how well) did she do it? This book explores those questions.

Chapter one ("Reading Oprah") introduces the aims and origins of Oprah's Book Club and outlines its effect on publishing and its extraordinary and continuing impact on what Americans are reading. The second chapter ("Oprah Reading") places Oprah's Book Club historically in an American context of novel reading for both entertainment and edification, then tunes in to the Oprah show to hear what her audiences talk about when they discuss books. Chapter three ("Readers Talking") looks at what happens when reading takes place in public, in book clubs, and on a TV talk show. Confronting Oprah's decided focus on social issues and self-improvement, this chapter explores what the Book Club can tell us about the uses of the novel in today's world.

Chapter four ("Talking Readers") opens with Oprah's strained encounter with novelist Jonathan Franzen just before he won the National Book Award in October 2001. When Oprah chose his high art novel *The Corrections* and it became a financial success, she blurred the well-tended line separating high and low culture in the United States. The tension this brought out, when the discreet elite novel encountered its common conversational cousin, speaks to an American ambivalence about art: How do we judge what is good? How do we choose what to read? Would the defenders of democracy really let the people decide? The Conclusion argues that we have entered a new age of cultural democracy, when Americans refuse aesthetic authority and insist on an eclectic personal choice in matters of taste. In this age, conversation becomes essential as Americans explore, in various contexts and, increasingly, against the overwhelming force of marketing, what we like, what defines or inspires us. Oprah's reading revolution is as much about what she invites her readers to talk about and value as it is about getting them to pick up a novel and read.

Indeed, arriving as it did at the end of a turbulent twentieth century, Oprah's Book Club found itself in the eye of what could be called the perfect storm for talk reading, a confluence of trends as diverse as the expansion of Starbucks and Barnes and Noble, the rise of feminist and postmodernist literary criticism, the exponential growth in book club membership, a voracious, TV-centered self-help culture, a worldwide move toward democracy, and a uniquely American Culture War. There, at the center, were readers talking to one another. In coffee shops, around watercoolers, at PTA meetings, on airplanes, and on crowded beaches all over the United States., readers were talking about Oprah novels. As a teacher and lover of literature, I couldn't help overhearing—and joining in.

Chapter 1

Reading Oprah

So, three women walk into a bookstore. An Oprah's Book Club display dominates the space just to the right of the entrance. The first woman glances at it dismissively and moves past it to the New Fiction section where she spends an hour leafing through hardcovers before heading for the corner where they keep Literature. The second woman, steering toward New Paperbacks, pauses at the Oprah books to read the back covers of a novel or two. She picks one up and carries it with her as she wanders through the bookstore. The third woman looks relieved to find the Oprah books right there as she walks in. She grabs the latest selection and turns straight toward the cash register.[1]

As I have talked with many readers about Oprah's Book Club since 1998, I have found these responses typical. The first woman, a careful and confident reader, well educated and well read, regards Oprah books as supermarket fiction. She is *less* likely to pick up a novel if it's an Oprah's Book Club selection, even if it's written by a respected author she might otherwise read—Joyce Carol Oates or Barbara Kingsolver, for example. The second woman, also a good reader, though not so confident a critic, is a little overwhelmed by all the choices in today's megabookstores. She willingly takes recommendations from friends, book reviewers in her favorite magazines, or online discussions. She trusts Oprah's choices, generally, though she sometimes finds the novels depressing. The third woman, though intelligent and perceptive, might not be a reader at all if it weren't for Oprah, and she's certainly not a bookstore regular. She reads what Oprah tells her to and enjoys the stories, often identifying with the gutsy characters who overcome all sorts of obstacles.

I know all three of these women and teach many like them at the College of St. Catherine, a women's college in Minnesota's Twin Cities. In fact, in many ways I am all three women. A PhD in English, I'm expected to be the first woman, holding aloft the standards of literary classics and fighting off the destructive influences of popular culture—influences like Oprah, the Internet, and the mass marketing of confessional pseudonovels. But I am by inclination the second woman. I love to read what everyone else is reading. I can't resist a good contemporary novel, especially a confessional one. In fact, I study and write about autobiographical fiction. And I was born to be the third woman. The daughter, granddaughter, niece, and sister of (now former) Pittsburgh steelworkers, I got the sort of overcrowded public education that leads more often to a trade than a profession. I spent my teenage years with Victoria Holt romances and my grandfather's first-edition Zane Greys until I stumbled accidentally onto a Jane Austen novel in a stack of cut-rate romances at K-mart and became an English major at my state college. Of course, I also studied journalism so I could get a job when I graduated. And I got that job, but ended up in graduate school a few years later anyway, still reading novels. Now I teach and read novels for a living. Because I believe in reading—I believe that it can change people, that it can bring us together and deepen our insights about ourselves and one another—I was drawn from the beginning to Oprah Winfrey's effort to get Americans reading.

By now her influence is common knowledge. Confounding expert opinion about the decline of paper and ink, she tapped into an American passion for reading big novels. Defying the pundits who argued that everything was going digital, she understood that Americans were buying books, not just at amazon.com but at the now omnipresent Borders and Barnes and Noble Superstores. (Remember when bookstores were tiny and lurked in dark corners of the mall?) And surprising the literary critics, she has us talking about books—serious conversations about challenging novels.

Oprah's Book Club, launched in September 1996, operated at first under the radar of critics and professors. It was, after all, daytime TV.

Oprah Winfrey had only recently started to rehabilitate herself in the popular imagination, separating from the likes of Geraldo and Ricki Lake and show topics like daughters dating their mother's boyfriends (or vice versa). Leaving sleaze to Jerry Springer, Winfrey moved on and began using her daytime talk show overtly to educate American women. In a 1997 interview in *Jet* magazine she explained, "When I first got the job, I was just happy to be on TV. But as the years evolved I grew and wanted to say something with the show, not just be a television announcer or a television performer, but I wanted to be able to say things that were meaningful to the American public and culture. . . . I wanted to be able to use the show to enlighten as well as entertain, to have people think differently about themselves and their lives."[2]

Apparently, like many celebrities, she wanted to do good with the power and wealth she had amassed by doing very well as one of America's top entertainers. Because she had established her popularity as a compassionate and open personality, her viewers were willing to follow her lead from self-revelation to self-improvement. True, her ratings took a hit at first, while Jerry Springer's climbed, but in the end Oprah had read Americans better than the shock jocks. By the time the Book Club began, her ratings were back on top. Self-improvement was all the rage.

And self-improvement, in the American tradition, has always included reading good books. Though reportedly skeptical at first about the idea of an on-air book club, Winfrey's own love of reading led her to give it a try. She told *Publishers Weekly*, "I feel strongly that, no matter who you are, reading opens doors and provides, in your own personal sanctuary, an opportunity to explore and feel things, the way other forms of media cannot. I want books to become part of my audience's lifestyle, for reading to become a natural phenomenon with them, so that it is no longer a big deal."[3]

So, on September 17, 1996, Oprah invited her viewers to pick up Jacquelyn Mitchard's *Deep End of the Ocean* and read it in preparation for the next month's on-air discussion. Before Oprah selected it, this 400-page hardcover, a compelling though slightly awkward combination of whodunit and family drama, was selling well, though it had never made it to the bestseller lists. There were about 100,000 hardcover copies in print going into that fall, a respectable number for a first novel. Three months later, *Time* magazine reported that there were 850,000 copies circulating. By October 6, it had topped the *New York Times* weekly bestseller list, and it stayed on that list for an impressive twenty-nine weeks, much longer than most novels—and certainly longer than most first novels by unknown writers.[4] Twenty-nine weeks enters Stephen King territory.

The Book Club Begins

The enormous success of Oprah's Book Club took nearly everyone by surprise. Even Oprah didn't quite seem to get it at first. In the early days of the Book Club, the book discussion got only one short segment at the end of the one-hour program—fifteen or twenty minutes. *She's Come Undone*, the most popular Oprah novel ever, shared half the show with stars of TV's *Third Rock from the Sun*. Later Book Club shows were often advertised as issue-oriented shows, a proven format, where the issue (domestic abuse for *Black and Blue* or illiteracy for *The Reader*, for example) took center stage over the book. It wasn't until mid-1998 that the transcripts regularly began carrying the title "Oprah's Book Club." But in the final two years of the Club's first iteration, the entire Book Club show was usually unabashed book talk.

Generally, Oprah reintroduced the latest novel, played quotes from reader letters, and bantered with the women in the audience who, evidently (amazingly!), had all read the book.[5] Then she presented the lucky few who made up the smaller discussion group that month, the four or five people who competed for the opportunity to have dinner with Oprah and the author. The best letters—the most touching stories, the most relevant life experiences, the most astute commentary—won these slots. The taped clips show the beautifully dressed women sitting in overstuffed chairs in an elegant room, sipping wine and conversing. This literary salon, which began in Oprah's home and later shifted to a studio/study constructed specifically for the Book Club, was a central element of the Book Club shows from the beginning. As Oprah entertained her guests, presiding over the discussion, the starched linens, fine china and wine, she modeled how to read and talk about books and directly connected reading with The Good Life for her audience.

Interspersed throughout many of these dinner shows were issue-centered segments. Usually personal and confessional, these segments, though clearly linked to the novel's themes, were not always directly related to the novel itself or to its characters. Women dished about overcoming divorce, what we do for love, or husbands who lead double lives. And throughout the show, teasers anticipated the announcement of the next book at the end of the hour. When the big announcement came, Oprah unloaded armfuls of free copies of the latest Oprah book to the audience. On the Oprah web page (www.oprah.com), the dates of the Book Club shows were advertised weeks in advance, and an animated online discussion, often including live chats with the author, preceded and followed the shows. Readers who visited the site were invited to consider some in-depth discussion questions, posted as soon as the new book title was divulged, a practice that has since become common in publishing, as Reader's Guides with discussion questions for book groups are increasingly appended to many contemporary novels.

When Oprah announced Mitchard's *Deep End of the Ocean* and introduced the idea of the Book Club in the final five minutes of a show about pregnant women who use drugs and alcohol, she sent out a books-are-our-friends message. "This is one of my all-time favorite moments I'm having on television right now," she began, "you are witnessing it—mainly because I love books."[6] She spoke enthusiastically about reading, about how "one of the greatest pleasures I have right now in life is to be reading a good book and to know I have a really, really good book after that book to read." And she concluded, "This is the most fun I've had lately." Briefly, after a commercial break, she warned readers that the book is "really intense," and "not like beach reading." The phrase "a mother's worst nightmare" came up more than once.[7]

Still, *Deep End of the Ocean* is what most of us would call "pleasure reading." It's a mystery mixed with an insightful and captivating family story. Its prose is clear, its plot a forward-moving chronology, its characters mainly recognizable and fairly likeable, though delightfully complex (especially the older son). It doesn't wrangle excessively with issues—no Grand Inquisitor or rambling John Galt chapters here—but it *is* serious. What it does very well, in tone and sensibility, is grab its audience and invite conversation about plot events and moral issues—how families work, in what ways children "belong" to parents. Like many readers, I picked it up in paperback a few months post-Oprah, and couldn't put it down until I knew that little boy was found and safe. And I wanted to talk, especially to other mothers, about how it felt to read this book pursued by parental fear and doubt.

On the other hand, *Song of Solomon*, Oprah's second Book Club choice, is capital-L-Literature. An early Morrison novel, it meets any criteria for excellence that professors like me can devise. Full of fantastic images and rich allusions, introducing difficult questions about memory, community, and race, it followed *Deep End of the Ocean* straight to the top of the *New York Times* bestseller list. When it was first published in 1977, and even after winning the National Book Critics' Circle Award in 1978, it never made it to the bestseller lists—not until Oprah chose it almost twenty years later. Placing these first two very different Oprah novels side-by-side gives a sense of the scope of her Book Club project.

To Enlighten and Entertain

I first read *Song of Solomon* in college at the recommendation of my favorite professor (a philosopher, boxing coach, and late-night jazz radio host).[8] It was hard going then and hasn't gotten much easier in many rereadings and years of growing appreciation for Toni Morrison's exceptional gifts. I agree with Winfrey when she introduces Morrison as "the greatest living American author, male or female, white or black, hands down."[9] I found echoes of my own encouraging words to students in her introduction to the book (at the end of the first Book Club show, a twenty-minute discussion of *Deep End of the Ocean* tacked onto a program about the Collins quintuplets coming home from the hospital). Gone are Oprah's effusions about reading. In their place is the frank praise of a more serious reader. She calls Morrison "magical and lyrical" and claims, "She will make you feel and think"—what fun is there in that? Winfrey has difficulty summing up what the book is about in one sentence or phrase. "It's about motherhood and unrequited love and friendship and family secrets. It's about ten Oprah shows rolled into one book," she says. Most tellingly, she repeatedly urges readers to "stay with" the author and trust her. In an anecdote Winfrey has repeated many times since, she asks Morrison, "Do people tell you they have to keep going over the words sometimes?" Morrison replies, "That, my dear, is called reading."

The first book, then, is as much fun as Oprah promised. It's a pleasure read, though not a simple one ("not like beach reading"). A compelling and well-written conversation-stimulator, it centers on a contemporary white, middle-class mother in crisis. Other Oprah books, indeed some of the most popular Oprah books, share these same qualities—*The Pilot's Wife*, *Here on Earth*, *Black and Blue*, *Midwives*, *Tara Road*, *Vinegar Hill*, *Map of the World*, *While I Was Gone*, and *Open House*.

The second book is clearly a literary novel. It's more challenging, with an intricate, layered plot and more dense, poetic language. It features diverse, even strange characters with multiple motivations in complex relationships. Because it ignores conventional chronology and sometimes leans away from reality into fantasy and dreams, it often requires reading as Morrison describes it—that is, rereading. But, as dedicated readers know, the rewards of such efforts are profound (even fun). All of Morrison's novels are like this, including the four that have been Oprah books. So is Jonathan Franzen's *The Corrections*, one of Oprah's controversial later picks, and the Book Club's second incarnation promises to feature such literary novels exclusively. Like Steinbeck's *East of Eden*, the summer 2003 selection, any of these books might be found in a college literature class. In fact, the Oprah show about *Paradise* became a literature class when Winfrey packed it up and took it on the road to Princeton, where Professor Morrison taught the readers how to read it (in a memorable program I will discuss more fully in chapter two).

Morrison's, Steinbeck's, and Franzen's were not, however, Oprah's only literary novels. Several other Oprah books fit this category comfortably as well—Edwidge Danticat's *Breath, Eyes, Memory* (one of my favorites), Jane Hamilton's *The Book of Ruth*, Ernest Gaines's *A Lesson Before Dying*, Anne Marie MacDonald's *Fall on Your Knees*, or Maya Angelou's *Heart of a Woman*, one of only two nonfiction works on Oprah's list. And many others have been identified as literary, artistic, or challenging in similar ways—Andre Dubus III's *House of Sand and Fog*, Bernhard Schlink's *The Reader*, Joyce Carol Oates's *We Were the Mulvaneys*, Rohinton Mistry's *A Fine*

Balance, Janet Fitch's *White Oleander,* Barbara Kingsolver's *Poisonwood Bible,* Isabelle Allende's *Daughter of Fortune,* Ursula Hegi's *Stones from the River,* and Wally Lamb's *I Know This Much Is True,* for example. In fact, it surprised me, wearing my professor hat, to find how many of Oprah's selected novels were excellent in a traditional literary way—carefully written with attention to language, plot, and character development. Several were literary prizewinners.[10] Two writers for *Life* magazine noted early on that Oprah books "tend to outclass the company" on the bestseller lists.[11]

The pattern these first two novels set revealed Oprah's commitment "to enlighten and as well as entertain," simultaneously to meet her readers where they were and push them a little further. Both novels challenge; both novels please, but from distinct premises and in disparate ways. This dynamic, I believe, is what took the Book Club beyond a passing media sensation, like the TV book clubs that sprang up in its wake, to a significant cultural phenomenon. Here Oprah's role was not just the therapist/talk show host, the smart entrepreneur, or the wildly successful capitalist. She didn't play the perky cheerleader for popular fiction or the humble devotee for a well-known author. The Book Club placed Oprah in the role of cultural critic and arbiter of taste.

In my first Introduction to Criticism class we focused on these two primary functions of literature—to educate and to entertain. From Plato to Leo Tolstoy, from Longinus to Adrienne Rich, critics have wrangled over this sometimes contradictory pair in their effort to name what reading should do for us. And I have worked the contradiction with my students. Give them too much reading that is good for them and they abandon ship quickly. Tie it to reading that touches or amuses them and they're on board again.

The Oprah Effect

Clearly, Oprah's Book Club was the spoonful of sugar that brought many less confident readers to Toni Morrison. With Morrison's earlier novels, *Song of Solomon* and *The Bluest Eye,* it is easy to trace what critics have called "the Oprah Effect."[12] Both novels were literature-class perennials, long in print and selling steadily, and both took phenomenal leaps in sales as Oprah books. *Song of Solomon* had been selling at about 50,000 a year, until Oprah chose it "and orders exploded to 500,000 in hard, paper and audio versions," *Publishers Weekly* reported in December 1996.[13] And that was only the beginning. *Song of Solomon* stayed on the bestseller list until March 1997—sixteen weeks. Then, in May 2000, the more accessible earlier Morrison novel, *The Bluest Eye*, became Oprah's thirty-third pick. Two Book Club versions were made available in hardcover and paper, and the thirty-year-old novel appeared on *both* bestseller lists for more than two months.

Bestseller lists, following publishing industry protocols, are generally divided into at least four categories—hardcover fiction, hardcover nonfiction, paperback fiction, and paperback nonfiction. The *New York Times* adds a "Bear in Mind" list of editor picks, an "Advice, How-To and Miscellaneous" section in paper and hardcover, and, since the Harry Potter summer of 2000, separate children's lists as well. In the six years I studied the lists, I saw only two books appear on both the hardcover and paperback bestseller lists at once—J. K. Rowling, with *Harry Potter and the Sorcerer's Stone*, and Toni Morrison, with *The Bluest Eye*.

As soon as Morrison's novel *Paradise* was published in hardcover in 1998, Oprah chose to feature it on the Book Club (she had, she said, read it before it was released and waited excitedly to share it with her audience as soon as it came out). I compared the reception of this Oprah novel with *Ravelstein*, Saul Bellow's novel released about two years after *Paradise*, and with the three novels by John Updike published during the Book Club's first run. Most critics and literature professors, no matter their personal prejudices, would list these three writers among the dons of American literature, certainly among the five or ten best writers working in the United States today. Morrison and Bellow are Nobel Prize winners; all three have won National Book Awards and Pulitzer Prizes. So their new novels were eagerly anticipated, and all five of them were heralded widely in the press.

One week in May 2000, for example, I found *Ravelstein* on the cover of the *New York Times Book Review* coupled with a companion piece in the *New York Times Magazine*. For weeks after this *New York Times* double-shot, the *Book Review* editors encouraged readers to "Bear in Mind" Bellow's significant new novel. Yet even with widespread attention and praise, Bellow's novel, like most works by respected literary authors, never quite caught fire by publishing standards. *Ravelstein* showed up on the bestseller list for only one week—and at number fifteen. Updike's three novels, *In the Beauty of the Lilies* in 1996, *Bech at Bay* in 1998, and *Gertrude and Claudius* in 2000, never made it past the "Bear in Mind" section. Morrison's novel, on the other hand, spent not only eighteen weeks on the bestseller list, but four weeks at number one. There are myriad reasons for a book's popularity or lack of it, but a significant difference here was clearly Oprah. The popular rise of Franzen's novel in the fall of 2001 tells a similar story, one I will return to later.

In the first four years of the Book Club, Oprah's books consistently averaged about fifteen weeks on the *New York Times* bestseller list—paperback or hardcover books, literature or light reading, popular or obscure authors, male or female main characters or writers.[14] In the final two years before its hiatus and format change, when the Book Club met less often and the given wisdom was that it was losing popularity, that average *rose* to nearly seventeen weeks.

Oprah's bestselling choice, Wally Lamb's *She's Come Undone*, appeared on the paperback bestseller list a few weeks after it was selected in January 1997. It stayed there until October, then fell off and reappeared for another year, totaling, finally, fifty-four weeks on the list. By the end of 1997, 1.5 million copies had been sold. Another edition was printed, and over a million copies sold in 1998. When the Book Club featured a second Lamb novel, *I Know This Much Is True*, sales of *She's Come Undone* spiked as well, though the second novel remained on the bestseller list not nearly so long, at nineteen weeks. (Later, it had an eight-week run in paperback.) Even at that, *I Know This Much Is True* was one of the top fifteen bestsellers of 1998 with over three-quarters of a million copies sold, and nearly 900,000 in paperback the next year, according to *Publishers Weekly*.

Again, reviewing the *New York Times* bestseller lists from the time Winfrey began her on-air Book Club in 1996 until she ended regular meetings for a year in May 2002, not a week went by that there wasn't at least one Oprah book listed—not one week for nearly six years. More often, because she announced a new choice about every five weeks for the first four years, there were multiple Oprah books on the list. In May and June 2000, March and July 1997 and March 1999, there were five. During the week of March 21, 1999, Oprah books took up six of the fifteen slots on the paperback bestseller list. *The Reader*, the latest Oprah pick, stood at number one. *Black and Blue* and *Deep End of the Ocean*, by then in paperback and having their second run as bestsellers, were at number six and twelve. The three previous Oprah picks, *Jewel*, *Where the Heart Is*, and *Midwives*, were still selling at numbers eight, nine, and fifteen, respectively. The return of the Book Club promises more of the same, with John Steinbeck's *East of Eden* exceeding its regular yearly sales of 40,000 to 50,000 copies within hours of Oprah's announcement of it as her first choice by a nonliving writer on June 18, 2003. By the end of that week, Penguin Classics had 790,000 copies in print.[15]

Certainly a study of these lists demonstrates that Winfrey earned her reputation for operating the star-maker machinery, discovering unknown authors, and calling attention to neglected ones. With that as the given wisdom, I was surprised to find that several times Winfrey went for the sure thing, no risk involved. She chose Anna Quindlen's *Black and Blue*, for example, when it was already on the bestseller list. Quindlen, a popular former *New York Times* columnist, had seen her third novel debut at number four on the bestseller list of the *Times* in February 1998, soon after it was published. Oprah announced it as her Book Club pick in April, and it rose a little higher in the ranking, up to number two, the highest ever for Quindlen novel. It had a twenty-week run before it dropped off the list in July, returning the next year for a seven-week run in paperback.

Did Oprah influence sales of this book? The previous two Quindlen novels did not enjoy the level of success that *Black and Blue* did, but that is not unusual. Novelists usually build their audience with steady effort. However, when Oprah chose *Black and Blue*, it had already spent as much time on the bestseller list as either of Quindlen's previous novels, and her post-Oprah novel, *Blessings*, in 2002, returned her to the hardcover bestseller list for nine weeks, closer to the level *Black and Blue* reached before it was chosen for the Book Club. As an Oprah book, *Black and Blue* sold over 500,000 hardcover copies in 1998 and a million paperbacks in 1999, making it by far Quindlen's most successful novel to date.[16] *One True Thing*, Quindlen's second novel, was made into film starring Meryl Streep and experienced a spike in sales in 1998, three years after its original release in paperback. Even then it didn't do as well as Quindlen's Oprah book.

The Oprah Writers

The Book Club also picked an easy winner with Barbara Kingsolver's *Poisonwood Bible* in June 2000. It had already been a hardcover *New York Times* bestseller for twenty-nine weeks in 1998–1999 and a paperback bestseller for fifteen weeks just before it took on the Oprah "O." As an Oprah book, it reappeared on the paperback bestseller list for another successful run. Maeve Binchy, whose *Tara Road* was the September 1999 pick, Isabelle Allende, whose *Daughter of Fortune* Oprah picked in November 1999, and Maya Angelou, whose *Heart of a Woman* became an Oprah book in May 1997, were already superstars among bestselling writers and pretty sure hits with Oprah readers. Oprah's one foray into children's books, the "Little Bill" series, led her to Bill Cosby. Sure bets don't come much more sure than Cosby writing about children. Many other Oprah writers, such as Kaye Gibbons, Sue Miller, Alice Hoffman, Elizabeth Berg, and Jane Hamilton were successful novelists with loyal audiences before Oprah chose them. As Hamilton told *People* magazine, though, Oprah did for her what she apparently did for many writers: "Oprah gave me—and my books—a bigger, wilder life than I'd ever imagined."

So, while these writers were good bets for Oprah, Oprah was a jackpot for them. Chris Bohjalian, after seeing his novel *Midwives* hang out at a respectable 100,000 sales mark for a year, couldn't believe it when, as an Oprah book, sales hit 1.4 million, "dramatically, exponentially more than I ever expected to sell in my entire life," Bohjalian said. *Publishers Weekly* Executive Editor Daisy Maryles writes that being an Oprah book can move a novel from "well-published and modestly successful" to "mega blockbuster."[17] *People* magazine called it "Touched by an Oprah."[18] Better even than Powerball or a check from Ed McMahon, it allows Oprah writers to quit their day jobs and be writers full time. According to *People*, Wally Lamb stopped being a high school English teacher after twenty-five years. Jacquelyn Mitchard bought "a retreat in

Cape Cod," and Kaye Gibbons took a year and half off. Several of them hired personal assistants. Melinda Haynes moved from a trailer home in Alabama to "a house with a doorbell" and "more porch space than the trailer itself," with a BMW Z3 convertible parked in front. All of them became celebrities, at least temporarily, the kind of people featured in *People*. Jane Hamilton put it succinctly: "All these new readers gave me freedom. I don't have to worry about having a real job."

In my professional life, I often find myself surrounded by working fiction writers, in meetings, at lunches, over drinks at happy hour. In late August 2000, I attended a dinner at my college president's house to honor Elizabeth Berg, a graduate of our college and a successful fiction writer. Little did we know at the time how successful. Oprah announced, not a week later, that Berg's *Open House* was her next Book Club choice. I spoke with Berg a couple of months later, and she confessed that she already knew that night, but, as is the practice, had been asked not to tell anyone until after Oprah made her announcement.[19] So, as I engaged her in (sometimes suspiciously awkward) conversation about the Book Club, as she (suspiciously persistently) pursued the conversation, she kept her secret. But even as we spoke, huge shipments of books from her publisher were arriving at bookstores all over the country. As usual, bookstore employees were instructed not to open them, not even to peek at the title, until the designated day. It must have been hard for Berg to contain her excitement that night, but, even so, what I heard from her was no different from what I have heard over and over from working writers. They generally respect what Oprah does. And, in an age that has seen unfettered corporate gluttony and twenty-year-old dot-com billionaires, who would begrudge fiction writers more attention, more respect, even more money and fame? Who could blame them for dreaming (with an appropriate touch of self-mockery) of being Oprah writers?

The Oprah Effect, though very helpful for seasoned writers like Berg, was most significant for first-time novelists like Jacquelyn Mitchard, Melinda Haynes, and Wally Lamb. As Daisy Maryles points out in her year-end analysis of book sales for *Publishers Weekly*, "In fiction, veteran bestseller authors dominate [sales] and for debut novels a nod from Oprah is the only way to real success."[20] The only way. In 1999, for example, the only first novels in the top thirty bestsellers were *White Oleander* and *Mother of Pearl*, both Oprah books. In 2001, the last full year of the Book Club's regular meetings before the format shift, Oprah continued her practice of introducing at least two first-time novelists a year, choosing *Icy Sparks* in March and *Cane River* in June, both impressive first novels, and both deserving of attention from readers and critics. They both became bestsellers, of course, but like most first novels they might have gone virtually unnoticed had it not been for Oprah.

Oprah's Choices

In this continued commitment to giving first-time writers a forum, Oprah took real risks she didn't need to take. Here she made it clear that it was Not About the Money, Stupid. Oprah has never had any financial stake in the sales of the books she chooses, but her influence is courted by publishers, who constantly send her potential Oprah books. Though the process of choosing Oprah books is a carefully guarded secret, D.T. Max reported in the *New York Times Magazine* in 1999 that suggestions came from a variety of sources—producers and assistants on the show, neighbors and friends, even other writers. "But most of all," Max writes, "Winfrey reads. She told me her ideal weekend is spent reading three books, back to back. Staffers give the books a rating between 1 and 10, then pass it on to Winfrey. Her vote trumps all."[21]

Max lends credibility to Oprah's repeated claim that she chooses every Book Club book herself and also to her explanation for moving away from the once-a-month contemporary novel format—that she couldn't read enough books to find the ones she was passionate about on that schedule. By the time she signed off the monthly book club, publishers had come to depend on her support, seeking "Oprah-type novels," and, when they found one, shipping it "to everybody they knew at Harpo [Oprah's production company]." There were certainly plenty of Oprah-type novels out there, moderately successful contemporary novels by or about diverse women, novels that had Oprah written all over them.

For that matter, there were and are plenty of nonfiction self-help books that Oprah sends her viewers running to the bookstores for—

Simple Abundance, Talking Dirty with the Queen of Clean or anything by Dr. Phil. Books like these, what *Publishers Weekly*'s Daisy Maryles called "the familiar balance of spiritual solace, health, comics, and computer instruction," dominated the trade paperback market for years, as I mentioned in the Introduction.[22] In 1997, the first full year of Oprah's Book Club, things changed. Maryles noted in her year-end report that there was more fiction among the bestsellers than she had seen in decades— five novels in the top twelve, four of which were Oprah books. By 1999, with *The Pilot's Wife* at number one, there were more novels than self-help books in the top twelve—again, the first time ever the editors could remember seeing this. Here is clear evidence that Oprah influenced America's reading habits, nudging readers toward thoughtful fiction.

As with her selection of first novels and her choice of fiction over self-help, another arena where Oprah took notable risks with the Book Club was in opting regularly for novels by African American writers. Until Alice Walker made waves in the late seventies with *The Color Purple* and Terry McMillan hit it big with *Waiting to Exhale* in 1992, works by African American writers were rarely seen as potential blockbusters. With *Exhale, How Stella Got Her Groove Back* in 1996, and *A Day Late and a Dollar Short* in 2001, McMillan changed that. Accompanied later by two black male writers, E. Lynn Harris and Eric Jerome Dickey, she joined the band of writers whose novels would inevitably become bestsellers. Stephen King, for example, has had a top twenty bestseller every year but one since 1979, and Danielle Steel has not missed a year since 1982. Like King, she sometimes has more than one among the yearly top sellers. Robert Ludlam, John Grisham, Mary Higgins Clark, Tom Clancy, Anne Rice, Michael Crichton, and Patricia Cornwell all regularly contribute to the yearly fiction top twenty (and dominate mass market sales, those smaller paperbacks you find in the grocery store).

When McMillan, too, became a sure thing, publishers began to look again at African American writers, assessing their crossover appeal to white audiences. And, while there have been notable recent successes, Toni Morrison is the only African American woman to follow McMillan into the annual top twenty since 1997. Morrison, a decidedly erudite writer, seems an anomaly in the company of Steel and Ludlam.

But her presence there makes sense in the context of Oprah's Book Club. Except for McMillan, the only African American woman novelists appearing regularly on the bestseller lists during the Book Club's first six years were, like Morrison, Oprah writers. Evidently, Oprah not only introduced her writers to new audiences, she introduced her largely white audience to new writers.

And with modest success. Among Oprah's first fory-five Book Club picks, eleven were by African-American writers. Of those, four were Toni Morrison novels, one was Maya Angelou's nonfiction memoir, and one was Cosby's "Little Bill" series of children's books, all quite popular. The remaining five novels, *River, Cross My Heart* by Breena Clark, *What Looks Like Crazy on an Ordinary Day* by Pearl Cleage, *Breath, Eyes, Memory* by Edwidge Danticat, *A Lesson Before Dying* by Ernest Gaines, and *Cane River* by Lalita Tademy were less well-known. They stand out in the company of other Oprah books, especially in their serious treatment of social issues, including racism and slavery. And they have been less popular by Oprah's Book Club standards. Each spent twelve weeks or fewer on the *New York Times* bestseller list, though Oprah books generally averaged seventeen. Each totaled between half a million and three-quarters of a million in sales, while Oprah books averaged 1.2 million.[23] Still, for a largely white audience in an industry dominated by white writers, this is a significant inroad and one that demonstrates, again, that Oprah had a meaningful agenda for the Book Club. She could have focused on light fiction by well-known writers and created blockbusters every time. She could have stuck with nonfiction self-help and been influential. She could have played to the comfort zone of a white, middle-class audience. But she didn't.

What Women Want

Then there's the question of gender. When presidential candidates Al Gore and George W. Bush visited Oprah's show in September 2000, they cemented the perception that to reach U.S. women, you have to go through Oprah. And this isn't just the much ballyhooed soccer mom constituency. Oprah's audiences cross class and race boundaries, and her

Chicago-based shows always feature a multiracial, though largely single-gender, audience.

The Book Club choices reflect this demographic. Of her first forty-five Book Club books, thirty-five were by women—twenty-four by white North American women, nine by African American women, one by Moroccan Malika Oufkir, and one by Chilean Isabelle Allende. Of the nine novels by men (excluding, for the sake of clarity, Cosby's three Little Bill books), seven feature a woman central character or narrator. Settings range from rural to urban (leaning rural), U.S. (leaning South) to international (including Europe, South America, South Asia, Africa, Caribbean). But some topics recur—love, motherhood, friendship, self-discovery, overcoming adversity, negotiating difference, surviving.[24] It's fair to say that Oprah novels are, in general, by, about, and for women. But not women in a narrow sense, as in "not men," as in Freud's (and Mel Gibson's) famous question: "What do women want?" Instead, Oprah books capture the spirit of the old feminist maxim "Women are people too," the maxim that insists that women's lives and desires, like men's, are complex. Oprah books aim big. They aim for an audience that looks like Oprah's audience—women of all colors, classes, ages, and shapes, women who read and those who just picked up a novel for the first time in years, women like the three I described earlier. But, then, the novel has always been something of a women's genre, in ways I will discuss in chapter two.

Aiming for an audience of women has always been a wise move in the world of novels—if you want to sell books. Elaine Showalter, a leading feminist scholar, speculates that women buy at least 75 percent of novels sold.[25] But if it's critical success you're looking for, your chances are not so good if you're a woman novelist. An avid reader of book reviews, I have observed that the critics' lists of the top summer reads, the top Christmas books, and the top 100 books of the past century seem predominantly white and predominantly male—and often unpopular. I suspect some of the popular ones may even be what one writer calls "the emperor's new book," books everyone buys but no one reads.[26] To be fair, a few Oprah books might also fit that category. How many people, even with all of Oprah's help, actually finished the difficult *Paradise?*

For me, book reviews are a revealing barometer of U.S. culture. Since novels were first published here, women have dominated American fiction. Literary historians have pointed out that the first American novels, most of the historical all-time bestsellers (*Uncle Tom's Cabin, Gone with the Wind, Peyton Place*), and the biggest moneymakers were nearly all by women. We buy more novels, read more novels, and write more novels.[27] But literature is one place where, even in the United States, more isn't better. More is worse. Less is better. While commercial literary success has been largely a feminine sphere, excellence has traditionally been defined as *the lack of commercial success*—and it has been defined as masculine.[28]

For some reason, there has been a chasm between what we read—for pleasure, for fun, for entertainment—and what we value, critically praise, or teach in literature classes. Feminist literary historians and critics have spent the past thirty years explaining the circumstances that created this contradiction. It is clear that educated European-American men, especially easterners, controlled the publishing industry, held the critical clout, and ruled the halls of academia. Their tastes were obviously not the tastes of the general public, the immigrants, the working class, the uneducated. But their tastes defined excellence and characterized elite, not in some huge conspiratorial way, but because they naturally sought out what was familiar and comfortable, what they had been educated to like. And, as the Marxist critics say, they controlled the means of production.[29]

Scholars have explored the ways that all of us came around to their point of view, how we learned to see upper-class European-American taste as superior. And they have set to work debunking what we call the "myth of high culture." My friend Phil Snyder, for example, likes to repeat the postmodernist tease that he can teach critical thinking and literary analysis as well with restaurant menus as with Great Literature. In the best of all possible worlds, though, he would use cowboy novels. The point is, literary studies have lately been infiltrated by scholars who question traditional standards of literary merit, leading to the Culture War, a phenomenon I will discuss further in chapter four. These scholars ask why being popular would undermine a book's quality. Why is a middle-class audience roundly disdained? Why are novels by nonmale, non-European-American writers generally examined for historical or cultural relevance rather than artistic value? Why does knowledge of Shakespeare or Marcel Proust give you more cultural cachet than knowledge of Kate Chopin or Langston Hughes?

When Oprah began her Book Club, these questions were already changing the way critics looked at literature, creating a climate for women writers and readers unlike any we had seen before in American history. Since then, of course, with Oprah's help, the trend has become much more pronounced. Could it be we are finally carving out a distinguished space for women's talents and tastes in the realm of culture?

Yes and no. Sure, even car commercials have started to address women consumers, and, before the tobacco lawsuit backlash, cigarette companies were coming on to us. The government now pays for breast cancer research and generally makes sure women are included in drug studies. Chick flicks with Julia Roberts or Nicole Kidman get funding, if not respect, while women indie filmmakers get some respect but little funding. There are more women in the Olympics, in medical school, and in college. Political pollsters in the 2000 presidential election reported endlessly on the women's vote and how Bill Clinton got it, and Gore needed it. But I heard the tone that said Clinton liked us like he liked Big Macs—a tawdry popular taste, but not one to indulge if you want to be taken seriously, Bubba. And suddenly differences disappear, and soccer moms elide to "trailer trash"—and the demographic to aim for is privileged, male (acknowledged), and white (unacknowledged). The media aim relentlessly to attract that crucial audience of eighteen-to-thirty-five-year-old men, the *Jackass* and *Punked* crowd. Now why is that always the crucial demographic when we know that women, in recent years, have bought more stuff, swung more elections, and put *Friends* perpetually at the top of the TV ratings?

Not to go off on a Dennis Miller rant, but look at how the vast majority of the cultural elite responded to Oprah's considerable influence on what Americans read. Again, it has been years since we first became aware of this influence. But, even now, Oprah is rarely mentioned at scholarly conferences or in literary journals. There were more sessions about opera (three) than Oprah (zero) on the program for the 2003 Modern Language Association Conference, the conference of conferences for college professors in languages and literature. And my experience has been that when the Book Club does come up, the reaction is often patronizing or disdainful. After years of serious study of Oprah's Book Club, I could find only risk-inclined graduate students engaged in similar work.

Even in the popular press, the tone when discussing Oprah is generally less than respectful. While Toni Morrison claims that Oprah has begun a reading revolution, D. T. Max in the *New York Times Magazine* calls her "the most successful pitch person in the history of publishing" and focuses on "the therapeutical approach" she takes to her novels.[30] Gavin McNett, in the online magazine *Salon*, accuses her of having a narrow appeal—only to women. He writes, "it doesn't require much greatness of soul or much hard thinking . . . for an audience composed entirely of women to identity with the travails of sympathetic feminine characters."[31] So there it is. An Appalachian mother circa 1900, a teenaged black girl driven to insanity, a homeless, pregnant white women, a southern preacher's wife in the Congo, a middle-class British woman going through a divorce, an imprisoned Moroccan princess, or an Atlanta hairdresser dying of AIDS are all the same because they're all women. Have uterus, will travel.

Consider the spirit of the commentary on the release of the *Oprah* magazine in the summer of 2000. The *Times* consulted Samir Husni, a professor of media studies at the University of Mississippi. "Oprah is a drug for millions of women," he is quoted as saying. "They need to be reassured and told that everything is OK." No matter how often she does that, he goes on, "the women will still come running."[32] Now, I'm not a fan of women's magazines, but I have looked at this one, and I found it impressive—respectful in tone, addressing many and varied women. Nary an article about catching and or keeping a man. Nothing about plastic surgery, the miracles of Botox, or how to be more sexually attractive. If women's magazines are generally a drug, lulling women into ever-newer variants of traditional roles, Oprah's magazine is a bracing blast of fresh air. Take yourself seriously, it says, and take care of yourself. Trust yourself. Leave bad influences behind. Push beyond your limits and reach into the realm of possibility. Look at the Oprah magazine without a jaundiced view of the concerns of middle-aged or middle-class women, and it seems, yes, almost revolutionary.

Certainly there is room for critique here. Her shows are often sentimental and prone to episodes of hugging or weeping, and her Book Club choices were sometimes similarly emotionally facile, even shallow (I confess I have trouble defending *Back Roads* or *Jewel*). She blurs the lines between art and capitalism, discretion and consumerism. She is building a cult of personality. She focuses on identity and self-help, discouraging broader social critique or efforts at political change. Often she hearkens back to the earlier days of her talk show, appealing to the least common denominator. And, perhaps most unforgivably, she makes money doing this. Lots and lots of money. But, as Mary Elizabeth Williams writes in *Salon*, "Oprah, the microphone-wielding, diet-obsessed chat show personality triumphed where so many others disappointed because she was the one who never underestimated the public or its capacity for discovery."[33] Yes, Mr. Barnum, despite her flaws, she has gotten rich by overestimating the American public more often than underestimating it.

It is this version of a democratic spirit that carried Oprah to the heights of success. There is no question that she reaches people, especially women as diverse as the three readers who walked into my local bookstore as I was writing this. She reaches people and challenges them to read. And, better yet, they take up her challenge. My punch line, then, is this. Three women walk into a bookstore—and all three of them buy an Oprah book (though the first one didn't know she was doing it). And (wait for it . . .) you probably have, too. That's how she started a reading revolution. And that's why it is time to stop laughing and start taking Oprah seriously.

Chapter 2

Oprah Reading

The year 1996 was an important one for Oprah Winfrey. By then, she had been fabulously successful for ten years. Her Chicago talk show had gone national and straight to number one in 1986, and, at just over thirty years old, she had become one of the most influential women in America. By 1992, *Forbes* magazine listed her as one of the two wealthiest entertainers in the world. In 1995, word spread that she was on her way to becoming the first African American billionaire in U.S. history. But, if we are to believe the unauthorized biographers and gossip columnists, Oprah wasn't satisfied.[1] Even though she had bought her show from ABC television, started her own production company (the first ever owned by an African American woman), even though her talk show had been the most popular in the nation for years on end, suddenly there were rumors that Oprah was considering (gasp!) quitting.

She "was disturbed by what she saw happening to her show and [to] her many imitators," Philip Brooks writes in the unauthorized *Oprah Winfrey: A Voice for the People*. "Struggling to grab viewers away from one another, Winfrey, Jerry Springer, Sally Jesse Raphael and almost countless others catered to the lowest common denominator. It seemed every show featured cheap and sleazy topics designed to lure an audience at any cost."[2] As the celebrity-watchers tell it, Oprah was at a crossroads, seeing the format she had dominated going in directions she sometimes leaned toward and sometimes indignantly turned away from. She told a reporter in 1995 that her show was "trying to disassociate from the 'trash pack.'"[3] She explained that "there's a whole genre of television talk shows that I'm not proud to be part of and don't appreciate being lumped in with." But she *was* a part of it—or wasn't she? In the end, she chose to be and not to be. She would live in the world of daytime TV and remain a talk show host, but on her own terms.

"I realized that I had no right to quit, coming from a history of people who had no voice, who had no power," she told NBC *Today* show host Katie Couric that year.[4] In the midst of filming an adaptation of Toni Morrison's novel *Beloved*, Oprah said she connected with Sethe, the slave woman she was portraying, and recognized "that I have been given this blessed opportunity to speak to people, to influence them in ways that can make a difference in their lives." So she came back to her talk show "committed to not be subtle about it, just to use the show to change people's lives wherever I could, and do it, and just to come out and say it."

Her show took a decided (and daring) turn then, in 1996, away from the contemptible competition and toward social issues, spirituality, self-help, and self-improvement. It also took a turn toward books.

The Talking Book

Explaining the genesis of the Book Club to a *Life* magazine reporter a year later, Oprah returned, again, to her African American heritage and the written word.[5] "This is what I do," she told the reporter, after ushering her toward a marble sunken tub with candles on its ledges. "I light candles every morning to this," Oprah said, as she picked up "a framed, antique page of writing." The reporter goes on, "it's a list of dozens of names, each paired with a dollar figure. These are slaves. Every morning I invoke one of them with a candle. Today for me it was Rebecca, who cost $250,' [Oprah] says with emotion. 'That is where I've come from. That is the legacy that was left to me.'" The reporter concludes by recognizing the irony in "the woman worth nearly half a billion dollars" meditating "on a slave worth $250, who by law would have been whipped if she'd ever been caught reading."

In this world that Oprah invokes, reading retains the aura of the radical act it was, an aura that has colored the relationship of African Americans to Western notions of literacy for centuries. Because literacy was forbidden to slaves and their descendants in the United States even well past the Civil War, reading was a coveted skill, one that many black authors describe longing for in the earliest slave narratives and memoirs. Studying these accounts, Henry Louis Gates Jr., a leading critic of African American literature, finds what, for me, is a fascinating source for Oprah's talk reading and for Morrison's assertion, cited as the epigraph to this book, that talking about novels is essential to their full realization as novels. Professor Gates identifies "the talking book" as "the ur-trope of the Anglo-African tradition," tracing it to a slave narrative first published in 1770, the narrative of James Albert Ukawsaw Gronniosaw.[6]

Gates writes about an evocative scene from this memoir in which Gronniosaw watches his master reading prayers for the first time. He quotes Gronniosaw: "I was never so surprised in my life as when I saw the book talk to my master, for I thought it did, as I observed him to look upon it, and move his lips." Later, when no one is looking, Gronniosaw opens the book himself: "and put my ear down close upon it, in great hopes that it would say something to me; but I was very sorry, and greatly disappointed, when I found that it would not speak." Gates traces this trope of the talking book through several other slave stories, demonstrating the necessity for black writers of "inscribing their *voices* in the written word" [emphasis mine]. Gates argues that in a historical context of oppression, African Americans were seen as fully human only when they added a more Western mastery of the written word to their mastery of oral traditions.[7]

Oprah, the nation's most famous talker and now its most outspoken advocate for reading, aptly embodies the seriousness of this blending of the oral and written for African Americans. Toni Morrison says of Oprah's Indiana farmhouse that "except for other writers', I have very seldom seen a home with so many books—all kinds of books, handled and read books. She's a genuine reader, not a decorative one. She's a carnivorous reader."[8] Little wonder, then, that at the precise moment when Oprah tightened the focus of her talk show onto social responsibility, when she let that focus redirect and reenergize her show, she would seize that same moment to embark on a national reading project.

The connection between social responsibility and literature must also have been self-evident for Oprah, who grew up immersed in texts from the Anglo-African literary tradition, which holds this connection as another of its defining characteristics. She recalls reciting poetry by Langston Hughes, James Weldon Johnson, and Nikki Giovanni, performing scenes from Margaret Walker's *Jubilee*, and reciting Sojourner Truth's "Ain't I a Woman?" speech. She claims on her website that her "top three favorite books of all time" are *The Bluest Eye*, *The Grapes of Wrath*, and *To Kill a Mockingbird*, followed closely by *Their Eyes Were Watching God*, *Jubilee*, *The Color Purple*, and *I Know Why the Caged Bird Sings*.[9]

The common thread in these choices is that they have overt social justice agendas. Books like these, by and large, run counter to the traditional Western literary mainstream, which places more value on the apolitical, on a standard of aesthetic merit built on beautiful language, complex structure, universal themes, and emotional and political restraint. By more popular standards, standards that many of my students hold, socially engaged novels are sometimes dismissed as depressing. But though they depict and disapprove of injustice, they are not, generally, pessimistic. They "usually stem from belief in the possibility of improvement, and many . . . either imply or explicitly convey their authors' visions and dreams of constructive change," as Professor Elaine Hedges of Towson State University once explained.[10] In other words, why bother to point out a problem if you don't believe that doing so can change things? As Oprah told *Good Housekeeping* magazine, these books gave her hope. "Books showed me there were possibilities in life, that there were actually people like me living in a world I could not only aspire to but attain. . . . For me, [reading] was the open door."[11] So Oprah's aim to use her talk show to engage social issues and inspire self-improvement, to "change people's lives wherever [she] could," would naturally be tied to the books she loved—the books with a similar aim.

The Way West

In striking out for this territory, however, Oprah wasn't traveling alone, nor was she treading new ground. American history is an enthusiastic chronicle of self-improvement, facing west, with a book in its back pocket.[12] Taking recent historical studies in quirky combination, it becomes apparent that early Americans were much more likely to own books than guns.[13] And they treasured their books, packing them up and bringing them along in trunks and knapsacks when they left other treasures behind.

In *Revolution and the Word*, literary historian Cathy Davidson affirms that literacy has long been a primary value for Americans. "In a democracy especially," she writes, "literacy becomes almost a matter of principle, a test of the moral fiber of a nation."[14] More kids reading by third grade means that we can more proudly claim our rightful, respected place as the best nation in the world, or so the politicians proclaim to loud applause. Though few people have read a Horatio Alger novel, most of us know that their pull-yourself-up-by-your-bootstraps message is the classic American story. And from Benjamin Franklin to Frederick Douglass to Jay Gatsby to Malcolm X, a program of serious reading has been our preferred path to self-improvement and class mobility. Reading in the United States is, in iconic terms, the way west.[15]

Look at our way of dealing with what many saw as an immigrant crisis in the early days of the twentieth century. Not yet 150 years old and still struggling to develop an identity, much of the United States saw potential disaster in the huge influx of immigrants. Just as southern and eastern Europeans and Asians were arriving in record numbers and southern blacks were moving northward, Manifest Destiny ended. The vast, unconquered frontier had been conquered; there was nowhere else to go. With so many potential new Americans coming in, even the formerly maligned Irish suddenly looked safer—at least they spoke and read English, and education efforts could be aimed at them. How would we teach these others to belong here, to fit in? Just when the immigrant issue was exerting its strongest political influence, when membership in white supremacist groups was at an all-time high, Harry Scherman, a forward-thinking New York entrepreneur, started the Book-of-the-Month Club in 1926.

At first aimed "at a well-heeled audience already cognizant of literature," the Book-of-the-Month Club got its early subscribers from the New York Social Register and college alumni lists. It soon became apparent, however, that its advertisements "fed longings for upward mobility" and embraced its editorial board's mission to bring culture to the masses, writes historian Joan Shelley Rubin in her study of the club.[16] Not just educated businessmen and professionals, but secretaries and home-makers, immigrants and workers turned to the club's program of self-improvement and cultural literacy. My immigrant grandfather, the one with the Zane Grey novels, was once a subscriber. This group became the club's meat and potatoes, to the delight of the progressives on the ed-itorial board. Professor Rubin cites the lectures of Dorothy Canfield Fisher, a popular novelist and long-time member of the Book-of-the-Month Club Board. Canfield Fisher argued that cultural training, includ-ing a program of good reading, would "enhance the quality of national thinking." In fact, it would help everyone, even the privileged, by saving a nation that "is shut up within a prison of prosperity where the older doors to spiritual and intellectual life are locked. If it cannot fight its way to air, it will smother to death beneath its material possessions."[17]

Resisting the rampant materialism of prosperous economic times and restoring or igniting a sense of cultural value were the underlying aims of the mail-order club for most of those involved, though the pri-mary purpose was always to select a few good books, make them read-ily accessible, and sell them cheap to whoever would buy them. And, like Oprah's Book Club, the Book-of-the-Month Club succeeded on the material level beyond anyone's expectations. As cultural critic Janice Radway points out, "From its initial list of 4,750 subscribers, the mem-bership grew to 60,058 by the end of 1927, and in 1928 it increased again to 94,690." Not only that, but it inspired "innumerable imitators attempting to market culture through the mails." In just a year it became, according to Professor Radway, "a significant cultural trend."[18]

The Middlebrow Novel _____

The mail-order book club trend of the mid-1920s also institutionalized a category of literature that has since become commonplace. The critics call it "middlebrow."[19] Sometimes aimed high, at elite literature or "high-brow," sometimes low, at mass market entertainment or "lowbrow," mid-dlebrow generally finds a safe center in well-written popular novels. Middlebrow is not what you usually read in English classes or find on

Great Books lists. But it is also not what you hide under your bed and replace with Michael Ondaatge on your nightstand when your smart friends visit. It's what you read with your book club or with Oprah.

Middlebrow was a new word for a new century. Radway points out that the *Oxford English Dictionary* traced the word's first appearance to a 1925 magazine article. Middlebrow in that citation was a group of people "who are hoping that someday they will get used to the stuff they ought to like." It was a class-conscious concept, one that suited the consumer trends of the upwardly mobile new Americans in the States in the 1920s.[20] As Radway writes, "middlebrow" was a term that "had to be coined to map a new taste culture or aesthetic formation, one that self-consciously appropriated the value of 'Culture' and 'the serious,' even as it linked those concepts and the objects that embodied them with new, highly suspect uses."[21] Middlebrow was, in short, quintessentially American. It was about selling class mobility by selling culture.

I recognize the category of middlebrow from my bewildered but ambitious younger years—the years of poring over *Thirty Days to a More Powerful Vocabulary* and *Looking Out for Number One*. I knew there were things I was supposed to like, qualities I was supposed to have if I wanted to be more like Mary Richards and less like the early Rhoda, but how to get them? How to traverse from low to high culture via middlebrow mechanisms? The answer was not in my self-help books. For me, as for so many Americans, the answer was novel reading.

Without novels, it would be hard to imagine a middlebrow literature at all. Poetry is usually seen as highbrow. That's why T. S. Eliot, a status-seeking middle-class midwesterner, pursued it.[22] Celebrity biographies are clearly lowbrow, as are mystery novels and other genre fiction. That's why they are featured in *People* and on the morning talk shows. (See Katie Couric's first book club selection in June 2002: a mystery novel by a celebrity.) In America, the novel as a genre defined the middle then went on to colonize both the high (finding its way onto Great Books lists) and the low (as detective novels and bodice-rippers). Like the term "middle class," middlebrow is a convenient receptacle for all of our determined denials of class divisions in the United States. In some ways, almost all American literature is and has been middlebrow (which could explain why T. S. Eliot moved to England), for the same reason most Americans insist they are middle class. Avoiding pretension and denying elitism are essential in a land of opportunity where everyone is created equal. These are our stories, and we're stickin' to 'em.

In fact, novels provided the means to blur class distinctions in the United States very early on. Professor Davidson, in her study of novels in postcolonial America, describes how novels worked to educate readers, especially women readers, who didn't have access to formal education. These novels of the early nineteenth century "tended to proclaim a socially egalitarian message" that women readers responded to eagerly. She explains: "While exploiting a sentimental or Gothic plot, the novel also regularly provided a kind of education that could even parallel—admittedly, in a minor key—that which was provided by the men's colleges." Novels, she writes, "often included Greek or Latin quotations (in translation or, in footnotes, conveniently translated for those unversed in classical tongues)." And, in the context of a compelling story, these books "also provided readers with clues for how to improve their vocabulary or writing skills, by using a variety of syntactic structures or sometimes even contextually defining an unusual word." Finally, the characters themselves take up the task of education, commenting, "breathlessly, on the beauty of another's discourse; the fine form of a poem or letter; the grace and strength of a clear hand; the excellence of another's learning, intelligence, and expression." She concludes that, "in contrast to the numerous contemporaneous attacks against intellectual women, fiction championed these women in a way apprehensible—and inspiring—to women whose own education (and educational opportunities) might be severely restricted."[23]

But because even women and the uneducated could (and did) read them, novels were also suspect from the beginning. And the uneducated did not just read them. They wrote them. White women and African Americans, with little or no access to formal education, were such popular writers in the nineteenth-century United States that Hawthorne and Melville tried to imitate them. Now *that*, later critics chafed, was too much. Evidently, novels were too blatant an assertion of democracy, of free choice without the mediation of the educated elite who had been explaining the Bible and poetry to us for centuries. Endless tracts in Europe and the United States in the eighteenth and nineteenth centuries began exhorting men and women, but especially women, to avoid novel reading. Conduct books and sermons repeat the message, and even the novels themselves take it up. There's the silly Catherine Morland in Jane Austen's *Northanger Abbey* who reads so many gothic novels that her view of reality blurs and she becomes the target of Austen's wicked wit. Then there's Rose, from Louisa May Alcott's 1876 novel *Rose in Bloom*. When she is caught reading a risqué French (of course) novel, Rose must be redirected by the wise men around her to the (fresh, robust, American) essays of Ralph Waldo Emerson and Henry David Thoreau. When she says her prayers at night, Rose asks to be "kept from yielding to three of the small temptations which beset a rich, pretty, and romantic girl— extravagance, coquetry, and novel-reading."[24]

It wasn't unusual for novels like Alcott's to make an exception for themselves, precisely because they were engaged in education. Davidson notes that "virtually *every* American novel written before 1820 (I can think of no exceptions) at some point includes either a discourse on the necessity of improved education (often with special attention to the need for better female education) or a description of then-current education . . . or, at the very least, a comment on the educational levels and reading habits of the hero and even moreso the heroine."[25] Novels are good, then, if they are good for you, if they pass the time usefully rather than wastefully; if they are about educating as well as entertaining.

It is easy to see how early authors and critics, like early novel readers, worked hard at negotiating a respectable middle ground for their new literary genre. They had to do it because they were not going to give up on the lucrative novel. Novels were a pleasure to read, especially considering the alternatives. As a writer in *Harper's* observed in 1853, "hundreds of readers who would sleep over a sermon, or drone over an essay, or yield a cold and barren assent to the deductions of an ethical treatise, will be startled into reflection, or won to emulation, or roused into effort, by the delineations they meet with in a tale which they opened only for the amusement of an hour."[26]

You couldn't beat the novel's "union of popularity and artistry." Their "provocative plots encouraged reading," Davidson writes. "Differing from . . . more traditional literary forms such as the biography, the history, the religious or the social or political manifesto, the early novel spoke to those not included in the established power structures of the early Republic and welcomed into the republic of letters citizens who had previously been invited, implicitly and explicitly, to stay out."[27] So, with the spirit of the age that saw "the emergence of the people as a political and cultural force," the novel became extraordinarily popular with "the newly literate masses" in America in the nineteenth century, according to literary historian Nina Baym. We quickly became "a nation of novel readers."[28]

In a fascinating circle, then, readers were drawn to novels because they were entertaining, while the popularity of novels drew more people, even disenfranchised people, to become literate by reading them. In this way, novels both attracted and constructed a mass audience, an audience that became, in the early twentieth century, an expanding middle class full of consumers of now respectable middlebrow literature—and book club subscribers. In short, reading, once the enterprise only of the educated elite, met democracy head on in American novels and, perhaps as much as any political force, launched the middle-class nation we would become.

So when, in 1996, Oprah approached her huge TV audience with an armful of novels and invited them to read with her, she stood on a foundation of novel reading that, in many ways, had helped us to navigate the century about to end. And she would ring in the new century with a resurgence of the same sort of middlebrow literature that had once engaged us enough to make us a novel-reading nation. From the first, she never said she was going to get the whole country reading; it was always "I want to get the whole country reading *again*" [emphasis mine]. And to do that, of course, she would begin with women and with the ever-compelling middlebrow novel. What could be more obvious?

The Middlebrow Book Club

Consider an exchange between Oprah and a pair of women readers, Cynthia and Melinda, at the second meeting of Oprah's Book Club, in November 1996. It was the dinner, Oprah announced, that she had been waiting for all her life, when Toni Morrison, "the greatest writer of our time comes to my house," a dinner she describes as "a life-changing night for all of us."[29] Over cocktails and crab cakes flown in from Maryland, four readers join Winfrey and Morrison to discuss *Song of Solomon*. Early in the discussion, one reader, Cynthia, hearkens back to the previous month when the Book Club kicked off with *Deep End of the Ocean*. Contrasting the first novel with Morrison's, she comes close to accusing Oprah of a setup. "But it seemed planned to me," she said to Oprah. "It seemed as though you led them in with *Deep End* and then . . . ."

Oprah interrupts, apparently catching Cynthia's tone. "Led them into the deep end and dropped them off," she finishes. Picking up on the metaphor, Melinda joins in. "Reeled them in is more [like it]," she begins, softening Cynthia's point. Then Melinda opens her book to show how it is marked and color-coded throughout, as all the while Oprah exclaims and calls the group's attention to Melinda's book. "I just wanted to show you what I mean," Melinda continues. "See what happened here? I mean, it's almost like every page I would have ended up having a Post-It note on because it all hits you." Going back to the first novel, she points out that, though "I appreciated the book, but there were not like . . .," and she struggles for the language to describe the difference between the first two Book Club books. Oprah defends herself then. "I had to get you in," she says. "I had to get you to wade in with me. OK?" And Melinda allows it. "Right," she repeats, "you lured me in. I appreciate it."

Apparently, Oprah had chosen to reel readers in (to borrow their metaphor) with a page-turner, to bait them with a book they couldn't put down (*Deep End of the Ocean*), and then hook them with one they had to work to understand (*Song of Solomon*). She begins, essentially, by leaning lowbrow, and then quickly shifts toward highbrow. Doing this consistently over the first six years of the Book Club, she delineated for her audience a range of good contemporary fiction. In effect, she circumscribed the parameters of the American middlebrow novel.

Oprah reveals as much again a few months later when she introduces *Stones from the River* as the fifth Book Club selection. By the spring of 1997, the Book Club had read the heavy but entertaining *Book of Ruth* and *She's Come Undone*, which Oprah calls "a little wicky-whacky-doodle," in addition to *Deep End of the Ocean* and *Song of Solomon* (see the chronological list in Appendix B).[30] When they get to the hefty 525-page exploration of German Holocaust guilt, Oprah openly hopes that, by now, she has earned their trust so that her readers are done wading and will "take the plunge" and "stay with" her. "OK," she says. "So let's admit it's not an easy book, especially first getting into it." But, she reminds them, quoting Morrison, "'That, my dear, is called reading.'"

Oprah is plainly establishing a pattern for the Book Club to both entertain and educate, as we have seen. With a new novel nearly every month, she set out, like the nineteenth-century novelists, to both sell and teach reading. Back and forth she goes from novels that her readers find familiar and easy to identify with (though, again, solidly middle-brow) to ones they find challenging and sometimes formidable. She wants them not just to read (though getting them reading is central) but also to *read*—with more depth, with greater insight, with appreciation and enjoyment. She wants them to "take the plunge" into reading critically. If they do this, she asserts repeatedly (and, I think, honestly believes), they will, like earlier Americans, improve themselves and enrich their lives. And she will fulfill the calling of her talk show.

Listening to her introduce the novels at the beginning and end of the Book Club programs reveals most clearly how she moves all around the territory of good fiction, angling for readers at every turn. Sometimes she is effusive, raving about how she couldn't put the book down, or how she woke at 3 A.M. thinking about the characters. She refers often to the fun the readers will have with her latest choice, or how they will identify with its situations. "You're going to love it," she says of *Here on Earth*, for example, "because it's going to remind you of some of the dumb things we've all done in the name of love."[31]

Then, sometimes, she is coaching more than selling, and her tone shifts from effusive to encouraging. She urges her readers to stay with a big book or to savor the language of a lovely one. For the Kaye Gibbons introduction, for instance, she advises the audience to read *Ellen Foster* first, then *Virtuous Woman*. "I would not mix up the order if I were you. There's a whole feeling you're looking for, and if you want that feeling, read this one first [*Ellen Foster*] and this one [*Virtuous Woman*]."[32] Or, preparing them for *Paradise*, she quotes the ad that inspired the novel: "'Come prepared or not at all,' because reading [Toni Morrison's] books is like savoring a gourmet dining experience. This is not like a fast-food read. It's not like a take-out read. When you finish this book, you will know that you have really accomplished something because it is a great journey. . . . Once you accomplish reading this book, then you are a bona fide certified reader."[33]

This coaching fascinates me as a teacher with similar goals—teaching students critical reading skills, making them "bona fide certified readers" (and, of course, changing their lives). I loved that the first live, unscripted comment ever from a Book Club audience member, in the *Deep End of the Ocean* discussion, was "I liked it a lot."[34] Perfect! I recognize that immediately as the place where we often begin in a literature class. And Oprah has a fine response. Like a good teacher she follows up, affirming the comment, and then encouraging more: "You liked it a lot. Were you apprehensive at first?" The response she elicits is revealing: "No, I . . . actually never liked to read before. And this has really gotten me interested in reading. I loved the book, and I loved what it had to say."

That the book had something "to say" connects talking and reading in a way that makes reading more accessible for this less experienced reader. This casual turn of a phrase speaks volumes about Oprah's Book Club. It demonstrates how Oprah lured hundreds of thousands of new readers in by showing them how books could speak to them and how they could, in return, have conversation with books.

Reading Lessons

Deep End of the Ocean

Once these new readers were hooked, however, Oprah's challenge was to get the more precise answer to her question, to every serious reader's question, "What did you like about it?" The conversation in this first Book Club meeting never quite gets there—but few first book club meetings or early-in-the-semester literature class discussions ever do. The responses we see are mostly "I identified with" the setting, characters, situation, or "I responded personally" to the main character, Beth. One reader/dinner guest even vehemently "just got tired of" Beth avoiding her problems, of allowing herself the "luxury" of a mental breakdown instead of dealing with her life as it was. Though Winfrey and Mitchard push the conversation, asking, "Do you think parents have favorites?"

and quoting the book ("How could I love my heart more than my brain?"), the tone of this first Book Club meeting as we come to see it—edited down to a few concise clips for TV—is all about bonding and identifying. We observe the readers reading the characters as if they are real people. And Oprah's questions invite them to consider how the book affects them emotionally, not so much what it makes them think about or what questions it raises for them.

As an English professor, it's my job to prefer reflective reading, reading that poses challenging questions and doesn't forget that novels are fictional constructions (stories, even lies). But I see reading for connection and affect as a legitimate way of reading, too. I have been in book groups that employed these skills, mainly of responding to characters as people, of applying human insights to books. Doing so allowed us to approach books realistically and on even ground despite differing levels of experience with reading—we had all observed people, and we could all talk about them. And talking about fictional people doesn't count as gossip, right? Reading like this also opens avenues to intimacy, to establishing stronger relationships among the members of a group—which, after all, is at least half the point of getting together, as sociologist Elizabeth Long has shown in her remarkable work on women's book clubs.[35] Moreover, as feminist psychologists have pointed out, connection and identification are modes that women in American culture generally employ comfortably.[36]

For any reader, connecting to characters as people is a useful skill that often allows striking insights. I know many journalists and English professors who credit an early and passionate identification with Jo March, the tomboy-author in *Little Women*, with making them lifelong lovers of the written word. As a middle-aged woman, I still haven't recovered completely from an intense connection with George Eliot's young Maggie Tulliver from *Mill on the Floss*. And even now, twenty years married, I wouldn't mind meeting Barbara Kingsolver's luminous Loyd from *Animal Dreams* over a candlelit dinner. This first Book Club meeting, aimed at audience building, at helping many different sorts of women get comfortable with reading, purposefully targets empathic readings. But apparently Oprah and I agree: there can and ought to be more to reading novels than this—more *in addition to* this.

And as soon as Oprah mentions Toni Morrison at the end of that first *Deep End of the Ocean* discussion, we begin to see what this "more" might be. Her tone immediately shifts from girlfriend to teacher. And when the Book Club meets for a second time, over *Song of Solomon*, the reading lesson begins in earnest. With Morrison's help, Oprah overtly leads Cynthia, Melinda, Aileen, and Celeste (and, of course, her millions of viewers) through an exercise in how to read a novel reflectively.[37]

Song of Solomon

Oprah begins by sharing her reverence for Morrison's work. "In the beginning was the word," she says, riffing on the Bible. "Toni Morrison took the word and created a Song of Solomon." She adds, "There is nothing I love more than an author who knows how to weave the words and take you into a story." Here the God allusion ("In the beginning was the Word and . . . the Word was God," the Creator, the Book of John explains) and the idea of "weaving" a story suggest foresight, craftsmanship, and intricacy. Oprah is putting the author and her skills forward first thing. Though in later Book Club meetings she tends to lead with social issues or with the effect of the novel on her audience (an empathic approach, as with *Deep End*), she nearly always came back here, if only briefly, to the novel as a work of art, as something created by a living, breathing author. In the Book Club's first six years, the authors were always invited to the smaller dinner discussion, and Oprah seldom failed to ask them where the idea for the novel came from or how they went about writing it. And, inevitably, that response was included in the clips from the dinner discussion featured on the Book Club broadcast.

Oprah reminds her audience, too, that Morrison is human, "a single mother who wrote in whatever time she had between raising two sons." With Morrison's presence, both human and god-like, established as the center of the novel, Winfrey then reinforces with her dinner guests the importance of reading carefully, reading attentively, and rereading. "And when you read your first Toni Morrison, you think, you say, 'Oh, I'm smart, I know. I've got a degree. Somebody said I am.' And then you have to go over it and over it." Aileen, a reader at the dinner, agrees that the novel has to be read slowly. "I couldn't skip a word," she says. "And I'm somebody that when I read a book, I have a tendency, before I know it, [to be] another chapter ahead. And go wait, oh, I just—I didn't read those words. I just kind of looked for something to happen. And with your book," she says to Morrison, "I had to keep going back and read every word. I just couldn't miss anything."

When Oprah asks Morrison to respond to Aileen's comment she says simply, "Most people do skim." But, the dinner guests insist, Morrison's book won't let them skim. "Oh no," Morrison replies. "I write over and over again—revise over and over again so that there's not a wasted 'the.'" Oprah then claims the teaching moment: "Not a word. Not a comma. That, my dear, is called writing." Reading carefully is what serious readers owe to a serious author who writes carefully. That is Reading Lesson Number One of the Book Club's Morrison dinner, as packaged for Oprah's TV audience.

Reading Lesson Number Two follows immediately after—that good books are complicated and multidimensional. (Remember Oprah saying, "It's about ten Oprah shows rolled into one book" when she introduced the novel.) For this lesson, Winfrey and Morrison converse alone. "Now if you had to describe this book," Oprah begins, "because it's so hard when I was announcing the book to the rest of the world, I couldn't figure out even how to—we sat in a room, those of us who had read it, to try to describe what is this book about," she says, uncharacteristically grasping for language. "What do *you* say this book is about?" Morrison's response is clear: "Well, I'll give you a sentence, but you know that if I had the right sentence, I wouldn't have written the book."

So if the book is multidimensional and complex, reading is about the effort to understand ("There is nothing, really, Oprah," Morrison says, "nothing more exciting than knowledge.") but not just about getting the big picture. Morrison and Winfrey continue uninterrupted to Reading Lesson Number Three—that good readers read for subtleties and for a feeling as much as an overtly stated moral. Morrison explains:

> Some of the messages I want to convey are pastel strokes, not the heavy, thunderous ones. But the willingness to take risks with one's own life. The willingness to live an enchanted life, a life where

things mean something, a willingness to see the other side of things. It's like turning up the volume on your life.

The voices of the dinner guests return for a few minutes to affirm the lessons, embrace the characters, and offer the ritual concluding toast: "Here's to books!"

Talk Reading

While the reading lessons Morrison and Winfrey offer in this Book Club meeting resemble the ones many of us learned in school, they also differ in significant ways. Students in literature classes all over the United States, at every level, learn these general skills of careful reading. But where literature classes usually focus almost exclusively on reflective, intellectual approaches, Oprah's Book Club, connected as it is to the *Oprah!* TV show, develops its own hybrid approach to reading.

This approach necessarily embraces Oprah the talk show host and the skills she uses to capture the women in her audience. But it also owes a lot to Oprah's reliance on Morrison, the writer and English professor, as her literary mentor. Morrison appears on the Book Club four times, the second Book Club show, the final one before the yearlong hiatus, and two more in between. Her influence on Oprah's Book Club can't be underestimated. Together, Morrison and Winfrey negotiate an approach to books and to reading that suits the needs of Oprah's multimillion-member Book Club. Leaping ahead a little more than a year to the second Book Club meeting featuring a Morrison novel, the critically acclaimed and bestselling *Paradise*, the coming-together of the distinctive gifts these two women bring to the Book Club is even more apparent.[38]

Paradise

Paradise is a difficult literary novel. There was no way the March 1998 Book Club could avoid facing that fact. So Oprah leads with it, confronting the novel's difficulty head on. She starts the show with a series of clips—of herself saying, "Oh, I don't get it"; of her friend Gayle King asking, "Are we supposed to get it on the first read? Is that doable?" and of phrases like "over our heads," "I warned you," and "What is going on?" Then the repeated teasers for the next book begin, and they are especially encouraging: "It's a good one, a lot easier and a love story. Almost every woman can relate," Oprah says. She reveals, up front, that *Paradise* was hard for her, too, and that she is on her third reading of it. But she doesn't back down on how much she loves it or how rewarding reading it has been for her. "Wise author that she is," Winfrey says, "[Morrison] knows the rewards are twice as great when we readers get to unlock the secrets on our own. And that is paradise."

So even though she calls this Book Club meeting "a class" and jokes about "Paradise School" being in session, even though it is held at Princeton University with twenty-two "students" rather than four or five dinner guests, it will be far cry from a traditional English class analysis, an "explication of text," in which the professor "unlocks the secrets." If Oprah is the example, readers won't know what to think even when they're done watching the program or visiting with Morrison. They won't have a *Cliff's Notes* summary of the meaning or lists of themes or metaphors and their referents. They won't know which characters are reliable narrators. They won't even know which one was the white girl. Oprah simply wants her readers to come away, as she does, with a way into the novel and the desire to plumb its depths, to reread it and talk about it. And, again, she trusts them, her mostly female, daytime TV viewers, to get it. "Now I can't wait to read it again," she tells them. "I'm gonna start reading it again, beginning with the first sentence." As with the *Song of Solomon* discussion, Winfrey and Morrison are not so much demonstrating how to read *this* book as they are talking about how to read, period.

This is made apparent in the way the clips from the Princeton meeting are arranged. The first one begins with a cacophony of voices, then Oprah, saying, "One at a time. One at a time." After a voiceover notes, "We all tried to come prepared, but who could compete with these scholars," the chaos continues. First one reader begins, sounding very much like an English major: "We go along in the contemporary religion that's dogmatic. . . ." Then Oprah calls her on her methods. "But aren't you the one who went back to the Latin dictionary and Genesis to figure this out?" And the woman replies sheepishly, "Oh, well, I need— yes." And again, another reader goes back to traditional literary analysis, noting that one main character was "a goddess"—"It was Mary and Jesus and Connie the goddess," she points out. Oprah challenges again with, "What'd you just say?" as her voiceover notes, "There were times I had to call a time out." Oprah's last comment of this clip is the repeated "Over our heads!"

Here and in other Book Club meetings, erudition of the college sort, both real and feigned, is dismissed, even mocked. My undergraduate lessons from James Joyce—that rain is always purification, bread is communion, and three of anything is the Trinity—would not be welcome. The point is something completely different. Reading is, again, something more. But this time it's something more than reflective or analytical. Good reading must also be empathic and affective. Oprah explains, "First of all, you have to open yourself up. You don't read this book just with your head. You have to open your whole self up. It's a whole new way of experiencing reading and life."

The next Princeton segment has Morrison reinforcing this message in an exchange with Oprah's friend Gayle King. King asks Morrison how to read a challenging book like *Paradise*. "I went to college," she says. "I'm really kind of smart, but there are a couple of times I would read a page three or four times," and, she implies, still not get it. Morrison tells her that to really read the book requires more than the intellectual analysis King is aiming for. "If you had read it initially, as a friend of mine calls it, 'read it to the bone,' the first time, it *would* have been possible to sort of, quote, 'get everything,'" she says. But reading to the bone isn't simply having "an intellectual response to the issues being debated here." What blocks readers from fully understanding the novel, she goes on, is that they don't have another sort of reading "vocabulary"—"It does require an opening up," she explains. When Oprah asks her to elaborate, she offers:

> I mean that you enter the landscape of a novel. You enter it fully. You suspend disbelief, and you walk in there like an innocent but who trusts, and you trust the narrator, you trust the book. It's risky.

It might disappoint you, but that's the way you go into it. And things that you cannot sort of fathom become instantly recognizable and knowable under those circumstances. You walk in. "Does this—is this really technically possible for"—that's hardly the point. You suspend disbelief of everything that might not be possible in the material world.

I must say that I have never heard a better explanation of what a novel asks of its readers than this one—complete with literary allusion and lovely language, offered up on daytime TV. In the exchanges that follow, Morrison continues detailing this ideal reading, intellectual and careful of fine points, attentive to complexities and subtleties, but also open to experience and feeling, ready to let go of skepticism and to believe the unbelievable when the novel requires it. "I didn't want to write an essay," she says. "I wanted you to participate in the journey."

And in that spirit, she never offers an explication of the novel, a final reading that would allow the twenty-two Book Club participants or the millions in the TV audience to say, "I get it. Now let's put the book away." Instead, she insists that she "wouldn't want to end up having written a book in which there was a formula and a perfect conclusion and that was the meaning and the only meaning. There should be several. If it's worth writing, it's worth going back to later." Morrison also concedes that she rarely teaches her own work because she doesn't want "to impose on students" who want a "fundamental and final reading—as though I had it."

Morrison's deferential attitude toward readers is not traditionally professorial—haven't we learned to trust professors to have and to offer that final authoritative interpretation? Some of my students still get frustrated when I refuse that role, which indicates that their expectations still run along authoritarian lines. Morrison's approach to reading here, however, is much like Winfrey's. In this *Paradise* Book Club meeting, it goes something like this: a little exploration of character, a hint about chronology, a look at some of the issues, an insight or two into the writing process, more than one refusal to clarify allusions, and *a constant insistence on openness, participation, and involvement*, a decided focus on the social aspects of reading. The meeting concludes not with closure but with inspiration, with Oprah's affirmation that "the rewards are twice as great when we readers get to unlock the secrets on our own." In the end, the lesson is not to rely on authorities, not to, in effect, "take a class." The lesson is to trust your own reading while trusting others to expand that reading in conversation.

Oprah readers are invited to engage in a process, to read both reflectively and empathically, in both academic and popular modes, and to talk about books. Again, Oprah is respectfully addressing an audience that is capable, aware, and ready to learn, but also ready to dish, to cry, and to bond.[39] On Oprah's Book Club, the educated reader greets the general or even the nonreader in a conversational middle territory—a little bit literature class, a little bit consciousness-raising group, a little bit motivational seminar.

Song of Solomon

Winfrey reinforces the singularity of this territory as we return to the conclusion of the second Book Club meeting in October 1996 and the *Song of Solomon* discussion with Cynthia, Melinda, Aileen, and Celeste. Emphasizing the larger message about books—that they change people's lives—Oprah says of Celeste that she "had a transformation" at the dinner discussion. "Because Celeste, Little Miss White Lady Celeste here," Oprah tells her audience, had said in a letter "I am female and I'm white and I make a certain amount of money—a lot of money—and I've never been poor and I've never been abused and I don't know what you're thinking that I would have anything to do with this book." But, Oprah reveals, by the end of the dinner, "it was Celeste who was crying louder than all of us at the table, as we were all doing at the table."

By the end of this second Book Club meeting, Winfrey has affirmed the lessons of careful, reflective reading, while still embracing with her audience the skills of connection and empathy, both with the fictional characters and with other readers, and driving home the larger inspirational message of self-improvement. Morrison, too, reinforces all three in her concluding remarks:

It's a dream of a writer who really wants to connect and you see it in small ways. And people compliment you or flatter you. But to have something important, truly meaningful, happen to a person who's ready for the happening and the key to it is the experience of reading a book . . . . It's not a lesson that said do this and don't do this and this is the solution, but to actually engage in the emotions, the actions and the company—the company of the characters who come alive if you're lucky. That experience is what will always be special in my life, what happened at your dinner.

From this second meeting and throughout the first six years of Oprah's Book Club, I always found Oprah navigating this singular reading territory of her own in all three modes—reflective, empathic, and inspirational. I can find examples of all three in nearly every Book Club dinner discussion. Of course, different modes take over at different times, often depending on the book. Morrison always "turns up the volume" on the reflective aspects of reading, while the white-middle-class-mother-in-crisis books I mentioned earlier elicit mainly empathy. Typically the Book Club moved from one to another. The discussion for *Stones from the River* was mostly inspirational, about embracing differences and overcoming prejudice. It gave way the next month to a mainly reflective look at *Rapture of Canaan*, engaging philosophical and theological questions. The empathic discussions of divorce and loss that dominated the Book Club shows on *Open House* and *Drowning Ruth* were followed by the primarily reflective, writerly responses to *We Were the Mulvaneys* and *House of Sand and Fog*, which Oprah introduced as not just a good book but "an A+ book."

This meeting of modes sets Oprah's Book Club apart at a time when a fiercely competitive job market for English professors has upped the ante on literary scholarship, forcing many teachers to emphasize the distance between "reading for fun" and "reading for class" and forcing scholars to embrace a language of academic literary criticism that is increasingly elitist, sometimes accessible only to a small group of savvy insiders.[40] With Morrison beside her, Winfrey leads middlebrow reading into the borderlands of these highbrow academic modes, to criticism, to delighting in poetic language and in the subtleties of narrative. Then she marches back confidently to comfortable popular modes, to identification, to embracing characters and life lessons, and to listening with her readers to what novels "have to say." And in doing this, she begins to map a social reading territory, a public space that had been increasingly abandoned in the last century but one that ambitious Americans once lit out for with books in their knapsacks—a territory we will explore further in chapter three.

Chapter 3

Readers Talking

After more than five years of teaching a literature class about Oprah's Book Club, I can still be taken by surprise at the vehemence of a student's negative impression of Winfrey's project. "She is 'oprahfying' books," one student recently fumed. "That's wrong!"

"Oprahfy." Now there's an interesting verb (I say to myself, breathing deeply). Oprah, like Elvis and Madonna, has become one of those one-word celebrities, the iconographic nouns of American culture. We have other grammatical variations on proper nouns—like Reaganomics or Reubenesque. But the "verbing," as William Safire calls it, of a proper noun is unusual, and, I find, generally reserved for the derogatory, as in "New York is being Disneyfied" (or Trumped). Oprahfying is not about celebrity or power as we usually integrate it into language, the nouns and adjectives about what someone represents for us. This is about action, about what Oprah is doing—and getting us to do. (I have even heard the expression "going Oprah on you," like "going postal," only confessional rather than violent.) In fact, the word "oprahfication" was coined to describe the titillating public discussion of the personal, the disclosure of private emotion for mass consumption on national TV.[1] As far as my student was concerned, books should be kept as far away from *that* as possible.

Even the name "Oprah's Book Club" suggests a shady talk show aesthetic that erases the lines between appropriate and inappropriate, public and private. It implies that reading has a social function, an implication quite different from the traditional, high cultural idea of reading as an individual intellectual pursuit, an implication my student sensed when she decried the oprahfication of books. Reading a book in order to join a TV discussion or talk about it with friends is somehow more dubious than reading a book alone then stumbling accidentally, in a smoke-filled café, on a kindred spirit who has also read the book.

Harold Bloom, in *How to Read and Why*, asserts this view, emphasizing repeatedly that "reading is a solitary praxis," and that "the pleasures of reading are selfish rather than social. You cannot directly improve anyone else's life by reading better or more deeply."[2] Judith Shulevitz, in her *New York Times Book Review* column, agrees. "Despite what your teacher may have told you," she writes, "literature does not make society better." Reading and arguing with a book group, she insists "has nothing to do with coming together and everything to do with breaking apart, with figuring out how to live as an independent intellect and a soul loyal to its own needs."[3]

Yet all of the book groups meeting all over the country as you read this sentence prove the wrongheadedness of this focus on the solitary intellect.[4] The effects of social reading may arguably be indirect—the reading act itself is still, technically, a solitary one—but studying social reading has convinced me that the choice of books, the purpose of the reading, and its results can be collective to the extent that Bloom's distinction between social and selfish becomes irrelevant. There is no solitary praxis for book group members. Even *how* we read when we're alone, what we notice and what questions we ask, is affected by the lingering presence of other group members' voices. Elizabeth Long finds in her study of women's book groups that "reading in groups not only offers occasions for explicitly collective textual interpretation, but encourages new forms of association and nurtures new ideas that are developed in conversation with other people as well as with books." By reading, and reading well together, book group members challenge one another to think differently, to think critically, and to connect, to build community. As Long concludes, "the activity [of discussing books] is quite literally productive."[5]

But the imagined conflict between the solitary and the social reader has concerned literary critics as long as literary critics have existed, at least since Plato's Socrates decided poets didn't belong in his ideal

Republic. Recently, however, book group members have added their voices to the mix, and the difference has taken on a gendered inflection. In *The Book Group Book*, a collection of essays written by book group members and collected by Ellen Slezak, Robin M. Neidorf traces the history of her involvement in book groups to her mother. "Before I knew what literature was," she writes, "I knew book groups. Throughout my childhood, my mother belonged to a book group, which met monthly at the house of one member or another." She suggests that, in her experience, women "are not only more likely to read literature, they are also more likely to seek out the ways and means to discuss it." Book groups, she concludes, "are made up of women."[6] Katherine Lampher, former host of a weekday Minnesota Public Radio Program (and an innovative community book club), led a discussion in January 2002 that arrived at a similar conclusion. Men read alone, her listeners insisted; women read in groups.[7]

Group Reading

The roots of this gendered attitude go deep into American culture and mythmaking. If, as our stories go, men lit out for the territories independently, women usually traveled in packs. The citified women of our Wild West legends, for example, were tea-sipping widows, schoolteachers, missionaries, or gold-hearted prostitutes. Surrounded by sisters, co-workers, and friends (and contrasting with the solitary, silent heroes), they were distinguished by their desire to connect—to talk, to write letters, and to read books. They were our first joiners, the original ladies of the club.

In the past thirty years, historians have moved the real-life stories of these women out of John Wayne's shadow into the spotlight, as they have examined what life was like not just for the women who headed west but for many indigenous and urban immigrant American women as well.[8] The result has been a shift from seeing American history as a procession of great men, to viewing it as a series of evolving and overlapping communities of diverse women, men, and children. Ready and waiting for this close-up were the myriad women's clubs that contributed profoundly to early American life.

Before the literary and cultural historians reclaimed them, these club women turned up only in the margins of literature and the background of old movies as silly sign-toting suffragists or overzealous temperance workers, as members of sewing societies or as dried-up dilettantes in literary groups, women who "come and go/talking of Michelangelo," as T. S. Eliot wrote.[9] In *Gone with the Wind*, you may recall, they were memorialized as the irrelevant and judgmental "Association for the Beautification of the Graves of Our Glorious Dead."

Literary societies and other women's clubs were strikingly popular throughout nineteenth-century America; they were everywhere, and despite gender role restrictions they were successful by nearly any measure. And they claimed a key place in U.S. history as initiators of social and religious reform, political action and cultural change, of abolition, prohibition, and women's suffrage. The women's club movement included political, cultural, social, and religious groups—and some groups that embraced multiple functions for their members. From working-class women in factories who aimed to be more literate together, to socialite southern aristocrats, former slaves, and Mormon polygamist wives, women all over the United States formed "improvement societies" to better themselves and their communities.[10] These groups mostly disbanded by the mid-twentieth century, though one Texas reading group cited in Long's study of women's book groups has been meeting continuously since 1885. The genealogy may have skipped a generation or two, but it can still be traced directly from those women's clubs to the consciousness-raising groups of the 1970s and the book clubs of the past twenty years. As novelist Margaret Atwood observes, "Book groups are to early twenty-first century America what . . . improvement societies were to the Victorians."[11]

In fact, improvement societies were all that and much more, but because the movement was, until recently, unacknowledged historically, we had integrated its influences without recognizing its origins. These women's clubs provided the structure for Oprah's middlebrow book club just as surely as the American tradition of novel reading provided its solid foundation. From the overstuffed couches and lush carpets, to the closely read texts and carefully prepared food, Oprah's Book Club, like other contemporary book groups, unconsciously takes on the exact characteristics of the literary variations of these earlier improvement societies.

In *Intimate Practices: Literacy and Cultural Work in U.S. Women's Clubs, 1880–1920*, Anne Ruggles Gere describes how these groups distinguished themselves from what they perceived as more masculine academic models:

> Gathering in one another's homes, libraries, or club rooms that carried a domestic imprint, clubwomen assumed a less formal posture than that enacted in the classroom. Academic discipline of the body was supplanted by comfortable chairs, handwork such as sewing or knitting, and the consumption of food and drink. These accommodations to the body never appeared in the classroom, where students occupied hard seats in lined rows, with the figure of the instructor often towering over then on a dais, and where handwork and refreshments of all sorts were explicitly forbidden.[12]

Using the minutes from women's club meetings, Gere outlines how clubwomen in these settings encountered texts in challenging ways, intellectually, imaginatively, and emotionally and on different terms from the mainly academic modes operating in college classrooms. In one excerpt, a Michigan clubwoman attending a meeting in 1889 confesses to being more interested "in the sight of the dear, familiar, new-old faces" than she was in the reading at hand. But then, upon reflection, she concludes, "It seemed to me that we as a club have benefited from our association, in the matter of conversations—of being able to think aloud with less timidity and with more directness. . . . The intellectual food proffered . . . has had often the effect to send me home ready to read and think like a philosopher."[13]

Like these clubwomen, members of contemporary book groups admit to being less than academically rigorous and sometimes more interested in one another than in their books. Long notes that "reading groups often form because of a subtext of shared values, and the text itself is often a pretext (though an invaluable one) for the conversation through which members engage not only with the 'authorial' other but with each other as well."[14] This dual focus, both on the book and the reading community it engenders, appears in most assessments of contemporary book groups. Frances Devlin-Glass, in a study of Australian women's book groups, reports that it is important to the women in these groups "to maintain their currency as literate citizens through group discussion, not just private reading, and that, over time, they generate energetic group-feeling that is book-focused."[15]

Book group members in Ellen Slezak's 2002 collection *The Book Group Book* support this claim. Edie Jaye Cohen, whose four-person book group from Atlanta wrote a shared essay for the collection, calls her group "the longest committed relationship I have been in as an adult."[16] Another of the members, Shelley Rose, admits that it is often as much a support group as a book group. "Sometimes we barely discuss the book," she says. Then a third member, Rita Wuebbeler, concludes, that "the book group has made us a deeply bonded quartet that loves to read and share books, ideas, stories." Hedy N. R. Hustedde comments similarly on her Iowa book group: "In the beginning, I think we joined a discussion group because we cared about literature. We kept coming back because we care about each other."[17] Robin Neidorf also notes the sense of community she feels, calling literature "a point of convergence between different reader's lives" and "a bridge between the disparate lives of readers and thinkers."

Yet, even while affirming this dual focus on intimacy and literacy, book group members in Slezak's collection are aware that some academic modes of reading reject this approach. Kathy Ewing, for example, distinguishes her group from women's club stereotypes, even while affirming their group connection: "It's the only place I have in my life where I can talk about writing, not just plot and characters, but writing. We're not a bunch of dilettante suburban women making up pretty phrases, wearing our best outfits, and trying to outdo each other in insightful comments."[18] Cindy Thelen and David Vick, also embracing the social and intellectual, contrast their book group with stereotypes, this time academic ones:

> It's interesting to sense people's reactions when you mention that you belong to a book club. By their tone of voice or expressions, you know they are imagining a stuffy group of pseudo intellectuals discussing a dry piece of classic literature. Or they're flashing back

to their English lit class in high school and wondering why any sane person would willingly re-create that experience as an adult.

Well, anyone attending one of our group meetings would very quickly have all of those stereotypes and images shattered. Our meetings are characterized by lively conversations (sometimes two or three going on simultaneously and almost always quite loud), food and drink (the more, the better), and laughter (lots and lots of it).[19]

Janet Tripp, a member of a Minnesota book group, argues, as I do, that the very experience of reading changes with involvement in a group. "Books have more to say to me since I joined my book group," she writes. "Previously, the conversations I held with my books were a quiet dialogue. There were just two voices, mine and the book's. It was nothing like the communion that goes on now—full of exclamations, impassioned pleas, confession and campaigning, enlightenment, and exchange."[20]

Tripp's description reinforces the language of "the talking book" and resonates with my experience as a book group member. My first book group was an eclectic bunch, begun by a biology professor and a journalist in Provo, Utah, in the early 1990s. We were part of the embattled left wing of that consistently conservative community, and we counted on each other to affirm what increasingly became our alternate reality. So when we met, the dialogue was fierce and passionate, raucous and profane, sensitive and supportive by turns. In that group, from those men and women, I learned to read a book "to the bone," as the women on Oprah say, to go beyond my graduate school training and encounter literature on every level. Since then, I haven't been without a book group. Though my Minnesota group is more polite, it has a communion of its own in our cherished hours of friendship snatched selfishly from busy women's lives.[21]

The Talking Life

Like the earlier women's literary societies, book clubs like mine formed to answer the novel's insistent call to conversation and community. As Toni Morrison pointed out at the *Paradise* meeting of Oprah's Book

Club, "Novels are for talking about and quarrelling about and engaging in some powerful way. However that happens, at a reading group, a study group, a classroom or just some friends getting together, it's a delightful, desirable thing to do. And I think it helps. Reading is solitary, but that's not its only life. It should have a talking life, a discourse that follows."[22]

Oprah's Book Club aims for this sort of communion, extending novels beyond their solitary life into their talking life where they perform a vital social function. Featured prominently on the Book Club website in early 2002 was this quote, attributed to Oprah: "Just read a book. You'll become part of a worldwide community of all people reading the book at the same time. So much energy going into one place. Fantastic."[23] Highlighting this social function of books bolsters Oprah's claim to a different kind of talk show, one that, again, does good while doing well. Early on, many of the Book Club shows even solicited contributions for worthy causes—a flooded midwestern city library or a southern prison's book collection. "Literature is powerful," Oprah says again in November 2000, introducing her latest novel. "It has the ability to change people, to change people's thoughts. . . . Books expand your vision of yourself and your world."[24]

Without a doubt, this social dimension of novels, their talking life, is what motivates Oprah's Book Club meetings. In this context, though, books are often deployed specifically in the service of self-improvement or social change. And while I sometimes find that admirable, I also recognize that this is what many (like my irritated student, my first reader from chapter one, and many of my fellow professors) perceive as the oprahfication of books.

Oprahfication

Though Oprah's Book Club programs seem relatively less guilty than some of Oprah's other shows of public displays of emotion, of confession for confession's sake, giving books their talking life under talk show protocols has its own pitfalls. Among them was a disturbing tendency I observed, during those first six years of Book Club meetings, of stacking the dinner group with readers whose problems were like the ones in the novel. This move skewed the balance that the Book Club achieved at its best moments. It loaded the deck for empathic, rather than reflective, readings of the novels. Thus, it tended to preclude a "Little Miss White Lady Celeste" reading of *Song of Solomon*—unless, of course, she could fly like Milkman. Sometimes, experience threatened to trump intellect and insight altogether.

Black and Blue

The Book Club meeting for Anna Quindlen's *Black and Blue* in May 1998, for instance, hosted four victims of domestic violence.[25] It wasn't hard to predict where that discussion would go. The guests talk among themselves more than usual, and questions like "Why did you stay?" and "Were you afraid to go home?" predominate. Nearly every response to the novel is a personal connection, and sometimes it seems that only Quindlen remembers they are talking about a novel. Fran Benedetto, the novel's main character, is invoked as a sister, an inspiration, another one of the survivors in their circle. The readers at the dinner, inevitably, find it hard to believe that Quindlen invented her main character and had never experienced domestic abuse herself. The grand act of imagination that is at the heart of good fiction was beyond the scope of this discussion, as were Quindlen's first-rate writing skills.

Then again, I find it difficult to argue against such compassionate treatment of a significant social issue as *Black and Blue* generated on Oprah's Book Club, especially since I have been involved in activism against domestic violence myself. I couldn't help being impressed over and over by the honesty and intelligence of these women. In this meeting, Winfrey willingly gives up the limelight to her five dinner guests, hardly speaking except to ask encouraging questions. Quindlen offers the powerful and fundamental insight that when women leave abusive spouses they "don't just leave a marriage . . . [they] leave an entire life"—family and friends, hopes and dreams— much, much more than economic security and their "stuff." And the guests are remarkable: Catherine, who was reading *Black and Blue* when she found the nerve to call 911; Regina and her struggle to be honest with her children; Donna, who left her abusive marriage and tries to mother Karen, who is attempting to work her marriage out. "If I could give you a gift," Donna says to Karen, "it would be one day of my life without the fear, because there is nothing like it." This was, as they say, illuminating television.

But this was a Book Club meeting where the book definitely played second fiddle to these women and their stories. *Black and Blue* enabled, even empowered them. Perhaps it inspired their openness and clarified their situations. These are admirable accomplishments for a novel. It *is* fascinating, as Oprah later says of *Open House*, "that a work of fiction can do that for so many people."[26] But are these accomplishments enough? What are novels for, really, and how should we judge what they do? Two views predominate in academic responses to this question. On the one hand is "the notion of literary texts doing work, expressing and shaping the social context that produced them" as Jane Tompkins writes in *Sensational Designs*, her now classic book about "the cultural work" of American fiction. This notion stands in opposition to the more traditional critical perspective, on the other hand, "that sees [novels] as attempts to achieve a timeless, universal ideal of truth and formal coherence."[27] This opposition has preoccupied many critics of fiction, especially over the past twenty-five years.[28] What do we value: the novel's formal aesthetic qualities—the language, the characterizations, the images—or the work it does, its effect on the reader, its active engagement in the central issues of our time? Can we (should we) value both?

Again, academic tradition would have us give precedence to the formal. In educated assessments of literature, the kind, for the most part, that I was taught in graduate school, too much attention to social context is nearly always seen as undermining a work's universality, its timelessness. In fact, politics and social issues place a book squarely, and regrettably, in time. The best novels, I learned, transcend their social origins and cultural location; they transcend time. I know of English PhDs (and one former university president) who claim they won't read a novel that is fewer than 100 years old. Contemporary (even modernist) novels haven't yet stood "the test of time." To my mind, this is ivory tower elitism at its worst, not only avoiding real life and civic engagement but also misreading the history of the novel, a genre that has always claimed a social function.

Open House

On the other hand, approaches that focus solely on a work's social context can overlook the qualities that make a novel a work of art, formal qualities like imaginativeness and careful attention to language. If the Book Club meeting over *Black and Blue* does not sufficiently underscore this tendency and the risks inherent in issue-centered approaches, the meeting over Elizabeth Berg's *Open House*, in September 2000, certainly does. Here, despite the presence of a respected writer with a wider agenda, talk of divorce sidelines other themes or literary considerations almost entirely. Here again, the dinner guests are apparently selected almost exclusively on the basis of their experiences. Of the six, all but one are divorced, and the one who isn't writes, in her letter to Oprah, of the devastation of ending a committed five-year relationship. All their letters reveal, in harrowing detail, feelings of inadequacy, abandonment, and loneliness. "I wanted to die," writes Candice. "I literally felt the will to live just flow from the bottom of my feet." Michelle recalls, "The day he said 'good-bye' with no reason, I felt my heart stop and my spirit take its last breath. . . . I saw the light in my eyes go out." Most of the letters address the book only nominally, sometimes parenthetically—one not until the final paragraph. A few weave it into their own experience, connecting and identifying with Samantha, the main character. All six, however, end their letters with a triumph—moving on, entering a new relationship, or reaffirming their own self-worth.[29]

And this is the story Oprah highlights on the program, in the discussion, in the prerecorded clips, and in the "Remembering Your Spirit" segment. This story, which is also Samantha's story, is the one Winfrey overtly solicited the month before when she introduced the book as "a break from heavy reading" (*Open House* followed Morrison's *The Bluest Eye*, Sue Miller's *While I Was Gone*, and Kingsolver's *Poisonwood Bible*.) While the novel itself is assuredly middlebrow, Oprah seems to angle for the lowbrow crowd, traversing novel territory now with a different twist, changing her *emphasis* rather than leaning lowbrow in her novel *choices*. "It's a book about a breakup," she coaxes the audience "and how it leaves you stunned, confused and prone to do some of the most idiotic things of your life. And we want to hear about all of those idiotic things from you." The line Oprah has drawn between her show and "the trash pack" of other daytime talk shows grays a little when she urges, only slightly tongue-in-cheek, "Give us all the embarrassing details—what you did, how you felt, and, hopefully, how you, too, found yourself again."

Despite this setup, the *Open House* show is, as usual, more pep talk than voyeuristic exhibition. Oprah and the dinner guests offer advice like "Think beyond The Dress; Give up the fantasy; Don't lose yourself." And the dinner segment ends with a toast: "I celebrate and honor you for the women that you've become," Oprah says to the six women, taking in her millions of viewers as well, "for taking your pain and taking what was a very difficult time and turning it into triumph for yourself and for your children and for your lives. Here's to you all. And [by the way] here's to Elizabeth Berg. And [let's not forget] here's to books."[30]

Oprah's American Story

This Oprah show, like many others, celebrates women who triumph over adversity, pull themselves up by their strappy sandals, and get on with life—with healing, mothering, friendships, romance, and, naturally, self-improvement. As one *Open House* dinner guest said, "About eight months [after I accepted that he was gone], I realized I was singing." She could have been singing along with the powerful women's voices in the upbeat theme song to the Oprah show. So prominent is this success story that it has become the stereotype of an Oprah Book in the public imagination: a woman goes through dreadful circumstances and triumphs in the end—ta-da!—a better person, a happy life. It's Horatio Alger feminized.

D. T. Max speculates in his *New York Times* article on the Book Club that Oprah's fans are "looking for her in the books she gives them to read." That's why *She's Come Undone* was the most phenomenally popular Oprah book yet, he says. "It's the story of an intelligent woman with weight problems who overcomes sexual abuse and a difficult family on the way to realizing her potential."[31] (My students, however, speculate that the appeal of *She's Come Undone* is more like the appeal of a train wreck. The novel's relentless victimization of the main character, Dolores Price, has readers turning pages in fascination, as one undeserved bad thing after another happens to this perfectly intelligent woman. Dolores, they decided, is the "Anti-Gump," because in *Forrest Gump* one undeserved good thing after another happens to a not-so-intelligent man.) But the question Max raises remains: do the Book Club discussions reductively reconstruct and reread Oprah Books as nothing but books about Oprah, our most powerful recent manifestation of the rags-to-riches story? Is the Book Club just an offshoot of American celebrity culture?[32]

Occasionally, yes. This was very clearly *Oprah's* Book Club, and the themes of the Book Club shows echoed the themes of her other programs and her very public celebrity life. Children triumph despite impossible odds in *White Oleander*, *River, Cross My Heart*, and *Ellen Foster*—and in Oprah's life and through her activism on their behalf. Women lose love and find it again in *The Pilot's Wife*, *What Looks Like Crazy on an Ordinary Day*, and *While I Was Gone*—and in Oprah's life, on her show (especially with Dr. Phil), and all over daytime TV. Seekers learn to trust their inner voice in *Sula*, *A Lesson Before Dying*, and *The Reader*—and in Oprah's life and in the "Remembering Your Spirit" segment of the Oprah Show. People of diverse backgrounds encounter each other in Oprah's audience—and in *A Fine Balance*, *House of Sand and Fog*, *Fall on Your Knees*, and *Mother of Pearl*. Mothers who tune in to her program and mothers in the books love their children and raise them well, despite terrible circumstances. And, as they do so, they affirm their own abilities—in *Jewel*, *Cane River*, and *Where the Heart Is*. The weak and powerless confound the strong and mighty in *Midwives*, *The Rapture of Canaan*, and *Stones from the River*—and, of course, in Oprah's life. The American Dream comes true again and again on *Oprah!*, through Oprah—and in *She's Come Undone*, *Daughter of Fortune*, and *Heart of a Woman*.

If the Book Club shows, like other Oprah shows, are thematic, this is the result, again, of their talking life—and, specifically, of their talking life with Oprah. The audience is given to understand that they see only a portion of a longer (I would hope less thematic and focused) dinner discussion in Oprah's studio study. And the excerpts from letters are always only a few among "hundreds and hundreds," sometimes tens of thousands of letters about the book that Oprah's staff reviews.[33] Good novels are rich in themes and characters, alive with images and ideas. The best novels can take days, years, even a lifetime to think and talk through. And Oprah often reinforces this point, talking about second and third rereadings, even as she directs her audience to the theme at hand.

"The rapture is always there," she says of *Rapture of Canaan*, for example. "You always have it and it's never outside yourself. It's always right where you are right now." This is, perhaps, the novel's main message, and it's also one of Oprah's favorites. She focuses on valuing yourself, on cherishing children, on having the courage to stand up for what you believe, on celebrating diversity and embracing others. "Accept what people offer. Drink their milkshakes. Take their love," she says, quoting *She's Come Undone*. These are Oprah's themes, just as English professors (and, thus, their classes) have themes—gender, self-deception, colonialism, race, family relationships, class, intimacy, ethnicity. And remember, too, that Oprah's favorite novels all have social justice themes in common.

Book club members will observe that even their informal groups have recurring preoccupations. They are the preoccupations of its members—because readers notice what we are used to noticing, often what we were trained to notice. But these preoccupations also demonstrate that any kind of directed reading requires parameters. What delights me (and most readers) is that a good novel engages the imagination enough to push its readers beyond those parameters. That's why book club meetings sometimes continue long into the night and why English professors notoriously diverge from the syllabus. A talk show, however, has to reinforce the boundaries, cut, paste, and edit to restate the key themes and finish in less than an hour. Is it any wonder that sometimes the novel gets lost in the process?

The Elegant Balance _____

Given the format, it's a wonder the Book Club works at all. But it does. In this era of proliferating book clubs, of CSpan BookNotes, BookTV, Fresh Air, and Charlie Rose, books certainly have a vital talking life. And at Oprah's Book Club (and with *Oprah!* in general), the women understand what many others don't—that the talking life is always the point. Not surprisingly, the discourse is "never about just the book." Oprah tells her readers: "That's what a good book does is open doors to other areas." So while the *Black and Blue* and *Open House* meetings typify moments when the Book Club leans too far toward empathic readings, Oprah's Book Club at its best dances lightly with the novel's talking life, not just among approaches to reading but through some of our most tangled contemporary social issues. Letting the book lead, it strikes an elegant balance among the personal, the social, and the literary. That balance was executed often on Oprah's Book Club—with Jane Hamilton, Joyce Carol Oates, Wally Lamb, and Ernest Gaines. And this balance made the June 2000 Book Club meeting, the third one with Toni Morrison, the finest one I observed in the Book Club's first six years.[34]

The Bluest Eye

In her introduction for this program on *The Bluest Eye* Oprah, too, calls it "one of the best book discussions we've ever had" and asks her TV audience to "put down whatever you're doing and listen." Looking directly into the camera, she invites disarmingly, "I try not to ask this a lot, but if you could just put aside your bills or tonight's dinner for the next twenty minutes or so, what you're going to hear is powerful and wonderful—especially if you are a mother of any kind of child."

How could Oprah fans say no to that? How could they switch stations even when she directs their attention, immediately and emphatically, to racism, a topic most Americans are eager to put behind them?[35] In a prerecorded segment that opens the show, Morrison joins her. "It was important for me to say . . . [in 1965–1969 when I was writing this] that racism, that kind of abuse on children, hurts deeply and it is devastating." Clips from cartoons underline her statements and bluntly confront demeaning stereotypes of blacks. With this as background, the early part of the discussion homes in on how racism works insidiously in dominant white U.S. culture to humiliate and belittle African Americans, especially impressionable children. And that often self-contempt is its most devastating consequence. These are not pleasant facts.

But, with inimitable style, Oprah invites the largely white, female audience to accept them as facts and to respond empathetically. "Regardless of what color you are," she says, "there are a lot of women who have defined themselves by what people think of them." All races and cultures, she adds, identify with Pecola, the book's tragic main character. And that response, that connection, makes us all winners, not victims. "For me, the beauty of this book is that Pecola, and all the Pecolas of the world, have finally gotten our day." *Our* day. I'm one of you, and you're one of us, Oprah is saying. We have all, like this abused and unloved black child, been hurt by false judgments. And just saying that together, reading this together, the millions of us can change things.

This insistence on connection, on not just analyzing but *feeling* the significance of issues, is an Oprah trademark tactic and an effective one when it works, as it does in this Book Club dinner meeting for *The Bluest Eye*. Compared with the other two dinners hosted by Morrison, the clips from this one center less on how to read well and more on what we discover when we do. Maybe because *Song of Solomon* and *Paradise* are more challenging novels, requiring more attention to process than the relatively straightforward *The Bluest Eye*, or maybe because many of Oprah's readers, with nearly four years of Book Club experience behind them, by then needed less help. Whatever the reason, this Morrison dinner is different in significant ways.

For one thing, the dinner meeting is a more dominant part of the Book Club program. This show spends most of its time in Oprah's library/studio talking about the book. Other than the opening segment with Morrison, there are few detours from the dinner discussion. There is little banter with the audience and no "real-life" segment (except the

"Remembering Your Spirit" piece at the end of every show during that time period). The tone is earnest and intense from the outset, when the four dinner guests—all women, two white, two black—model the empathic response Oprah invites her audience to feel.

To begin, Winfrey, Morrison, and the guests all share personal experiences connecting them to Pecola, whose longing for blue eyes is at the center of the novel. Oprah recalls a picture of her grandmother lovingly "holding this white child," and how that relationship led her to conclude, as Pecola does in a similar situation, that "you are loved more if you are white." Stephanie Goodman, a light-skinned black Harvard-educated lawyer, talks about "the paper bag test," a test that once allowed only blacks whose skin was lighter than a brown paper bag to enter the elite clubs in New Orleans. Julie Valentine recalls the contradictions she felt moving between her all-black church choir and her (almost) all-white private school. Ruth Hoffman, a white English graduate student and mother of eight, reveals how difficult it was to help her adopted African American daughter to develop self-esteem, to believe that she was beautiful. Diana Bliss deferentially offers her experience of being told she couldn't be cast as an angel in a play because, even though she was white, she wasn't blonde. Morrison chimes in with mothering advice from her experience raising two boys. She recalls showing them her "critical face" when they entered a room—inspecting them, as mothers do, to make sure their clothes and hair were right. She resolved to change, to let them see more often how much she loved and approved of them. She asks, "When a kid walks in the room, does your face light up? Let your face speak what's in your heart."

Morrison, ever the distinguished professor and Nobel Laureate, teaches here as she has in the other two Book Club meetings. But here the lessons are a little less literary and more inspirational. She emphasizes, as she did with *Paradise*, that "when you know somebody's race, that's the least information you have. You don't know anything. The real information is elsewhere." But here the insight is not offered as a way to read the book, as in the *Paradise* discussion, but as a way to live. Morrison also offers a mini discourse on virtue and beauty: "Of all the virtues," she says, "[beauty] is not one. The virtues are not the accidents of birth. The virtues are things you work for." She continues thoughtfully, "to be forthright, to be educated, to be in control, to be diplomatic, to be healthy, to be graceful, to have your body be part of who you are. These are things you can work for."

Winfrey highlights this, as well as Morrison's mothering advice, repeating, "Does your face light up?" and calling this the best parenting tip she's heard. Clearly, this Oprah show is constructed so that parenting and appearance are highlighted topics, topics that will draw hesitant readers in the TV audience to a "depressing" book about a neglected black child—no triumphs, no happy endings in this one. This book, this show, this advice is for *mothers*, Oprah says. Not just black mothers, not just educated mothers. All mothers "of any kind of child."

But that doesn't mean the editing leaves all the tough topics on the cutting-room floor. Again, the show begins with a hard look at racism in our culture. And the dinner discussion wraps up with a frank and sometimes discomfiting exchange about child sexual abuse. The women spin out from Pecola's experience to their own, quoting from the book and revealing their own complex responses to abuse. Placing this issue next to racism, coupling the two social issues with more self-centered concerns about parenting and self-image, Winfrey leads her guests to see the book in multiple contexts. But Pecola and the novel remain central.

With Morrison, Winfrey can't neglect the literary; Morrison is, again, Winfrey's writer of choice for reflective Book Club meetings. Though Wally Lamb and Jane Hamilton have also made repeat appearances on the Book Club—twice each to Morrison's four times—it is clear that no other writer exerts the kind of influence on Oprah that Morrison does. Maya Angelou, whom Winfrey calls "a mentor and a mother figure for me," has been on the Oprah show several times, but she was featured on the Book Club only once, for one of the volumes in her series of nonfiction memoirs. On that program, the discussion was lively at the "sleepover"/dinner, with everyone lounging in Angelou's living room in pajamas.[36] But it centered not so much on the literary aspects of the book, on reflective reading, as on Angelou as a celebrity and a mother, an empathic and inspirational reading. After all, in *Heart of a Woman* the main character and her son have real-life counterparts with the same names. Life lessons, rather than reading lessons, were the order of the day when Angelou presided. But with Morrison, Oprah gets down to the literary work of the Book Club.

She invites the audience to be attentive to Morrison's language as she reads a passage from *The Bluest Eye* aloud. She tells Morrison that her every sentence is amazing, that "there is not a time when I have come to your words when I have not been enhanced by the language." As is her practice, she invites Morrison to talk as a writer—about what inspired her book and how she feels today about the characters she created thirty years ago. She also entreats Morrison to clarify the main character's motivation: "Why did she have to go insane?" Morrison, surprisingly, answers directly, with more finality than she has offered in her previous visits to Oprah's Book Club. "There were no exits," she says. "She had no doors open to her, so she made a door for herself. That was her insanity."

As skillfully as Winfrey draws out Morrison's insights, she and her capable production staff capitalize on nearly all of the Book Club's most successful elements in this meeting. Here we find not just social issues, personal connections, and literary insights, but also the intelligence and dignity of Toni Morrison, the earnest enthusiasm and openness of Oprah herself, and an exemplary mix of guests who respond to the book both emotionally and cerebrally. And there is a superb novel at the center, one that can engage readers on many levels. There are moments in this dinner group discussion, as Morrison speaks slowly and deliberately, savoring as she does every sound of language, when television's frenetic pace seems stilled. I can't help stopping and listening as Morrison reflects on "the ravages of an unloved life" such as Pecola's.

And then there is the striking moment when Winfrey proclaims that "the world would be different" if everyone read *The Bluest Eye*. Now, I know a lot of people who believe this about their favorite books (I might even join Oprah in this claim about *The Bluest Eye*), but where else, in years of classes and study groups and book clubs and seminars and scholarly conferences, have I ever heard anyone embrace the social function of a novel so openly and with such *chutzpah*? *The Bluest Eye*, she says, is "a national treasure."

Sure, Oprah's status as a celebrity leads viewers to dwell on her rags-to-riches story. Sure, her ratings numbers demand confession and easy affirmation, and her format requires a carefully organized and coherent one-hour program. And sure, her commitment to self-improvement leads her to overemphasize this aspect of novels. But despite it all, Winfrey does good work with the Book Club, work professional educators and critics have failed to do on a scale anywhere near this one. Oprah is, as Morrison says, a serious reader, and in the time she has, surrounded by a different group of readers every time, pressured by ratings reports, and lobbied by publishers, she still manages to invite her audience to read seriously with her, to read with depth and empathy, with careful attention to artistry and issues. I have never yet seen a Book Club show on which Winfrey doesn't open the book and quote from it; she never fails to ask her living writers about the process of creation; and she unabashedly admires writers, exclaiming, from time to time, how much she'd like to be able to do what they do.

But no one else does what Oprah does. The TV book clubs that were formed when hers went on hiatus spend too much time summarizing or selling books rather than listening to what books have "to say." Some defer too often to the author, falling into simple question-and-answer format. They take themselves too seriously or not seriously enough, sometimes choosing what most book groups would call trashy novels. But mostly, they trust experts or enthusiasts to talk rather than readers.[37] On Oprah's Book Club, the contemporary author and the host are never across the table from each other or side-by-side confronting an audience; they are encircled by readers, sharing the discussion, sharing the stage. On the Book Club, novels *are* (I concede!) "oprahfied"; they have a talking life. In the American tradition, they "enlighten as well as entertain." And in the tradition of the novel, they enthusiastically embrace their social function.[38]

With her Oprah novels, Winfrey traverses middlebrow territory from low to high, pulling in readers, from the tentative to the self-assured. Oprah, the Queen of Daytime TV, teaches reading skills more widely and more effectively than the professionals, in part because she earns the right every day as she models life skills, even survival skills for her viewers. For many, she embodies the American Dream.[39] She comes across as a real woman carving out a space she can be proud to own in the middle of trash talk and daytime drama. Using her skills as a devoted reader, a careful and inquisitive listener and an irrepressible talker, Oprah managed to do just what she said. She got millions of Americans to join her Book Club; she navigated the novel's social territory with her cherished favorite books in hand and got us reading again. Reading and talking.

Chapter 4

Talking Readers

The Corrections

It could have been the beginning of a beautiful friendship. While Oprah was launching her Book Club in 1996 hoping to get America reading again, novelist Jonathan Franzen was writing an essay for *Harper's* magazine, dreaming of serious socially compelling novels and a mass audience who wanted to read them.[1] They spent the next five years pursuing a similar ideal down different paths—Winfrey taking serious fiction to that mass audience and Franzen writing a weighty book that America would read—a National Book Award winner and, as it turned out, an Oprah book.

Or almost an Oprah book. Their paths converged when Franzen's novel *The Corrections* became Oprah's September 2001 Book Club pick. Soon after, the two separated less than amicably when Franzen publicly expressed uneasiness about appearing on Oprah and characterized some of her other Book Club choices as "schmaltzy" and "one-dimensional."[2] Winfrey rescinded her invitation for Franzen to talk about his novel with her Book Club, saying, "It is never my intention to make anyone uncomfortable."[3] This was gossip worthy of *People* magazine and *Entertainment Weekly*, as well as *Newsweek*, the *New York Times*, and even *The Chronicle of Higher Education*. I, of course, observed the encounter with eager attention.[4]

Think about it. The pedigree on Franzen's book was as good as it gets in American fiction. Critics started calling it The Great American Novel even before it reached the bookstores.[5] The academic acclaim surrounding its publication made waves so large they rocked boats in colleges like mine more than a thousand miles from either coast.

Responding to the critical fanfare, how many copies did Farrar, Straus print for the novel's initial release in early September? According to the *New York Times*, 90,000, a generous estimate for a literary novel and almost twice the total sales of Franzen's first two novels combined. And how many more did they have to run when Oprah selected it for her Book Club later that month? More than 600,000, *seven times* as many as the initial release.[6] With five years of experience behind her, Oprah could guarantee that even an unsuccessful Book Club choice would sell that many copies, because, as we have seen, Oprah pulled in a huge group of readers, readers that critics and reviewers still haven't figured out how to access without her.

That's why my favorite part of this story is when Franzen suggested in a National Public Radio interview that he might lose readers, especially male readers, because of the Oprah "O" on the cover of his novel.[7] Monica Corcoran followed up with a story in the *New York Times* about how readers on both coasts were requesting copies of *The Corrections* sans O. "It make me feel mainstream to be reading an Oprah book," one woman commented. "I don't want people to think I have no idea about literature or that I sit home and watch TV all day." But surely these few "bookworms" who considered the seal "a scarlet O," as Corcoran wrote, could not put a dent in the number of new readers the Oprah seal would bring in.[8] Clearly, Franzen could only have feared the loss of a certain type of reader. Thanks to Oprah, there was a moment in the fall of 2001 when vast numbers of soccer moms and waitresses in the Midwest were reading the very same thing the New York intellectuals were reading. Corcoran's story speaks to which group might find that pairing unpalatable.

But this democratic reading moment was a revealing one for the Book Club, one that highlighted the polarity of responses to it. Love it or hate it, there was little space in between. Franzen, who seemed to enjoy being the darling of elite literary culture, an artist "solidly in the high-art literary tradition," as he told a reporter, couldn't negotiate the divide, despite his belated attempts in that direction.[9] After his Oprah's Book Club appearance was cancelled, Franzen quickly backpedaled on the high culture talk. "Mistake, mistake, mistake to use the word 'high.' Both Oprah and I want the same thing and believe the same thing, that the distinction between high and low is meaningless," he said in late October.[10]

What was lost in the media hubbub was that Franzen was not the first intellectual to respond to Oprah's cultural clout with measured enthusiasm, to grumble about the erosion of high culture in an MTV world.[11] The real news was that he crossed a line in questioning Oprah's economic clout, calling the Book Club seal a corporate logo. As novelist Rick Moody pointed out, "If you are being published by one of the big houses, you can't object that you are not commercial in some way: what book doesn't have the publisher's logo on the spine?"[12]

And again, who was (and still is) making money from that "corporate O"? Not Oprah. It was, from the beginning, the publishers who requested permission to integrate the seal into the cover art of their books and keep it on when the novels were reprinted well after they had had their day on Oprah, in fact well after the contemporary novels version of the Book Club ended. Oprah always does better in the ratings with celebrity and expert shows than she does with the Book Club; she willingly loses ratings points to continue its meetings,[13] if only, now, five times a year. Many writers, critics, reviewers, and publishing executives have been careful not to question Oprah's book-selling power because they are the ones who reap its generous benefits.[14] Even Harold Bloom, notorious defender of elitism (and bestselling author), rushed to claim that he, unlike Franzen, would be "honored" to be invited on Oprah (hint, hint). "It does seem a little invidious of him to want to have it both ways," Bloom said, "to want the benefits of it and not jeopardize his high aesthetic standing."[15]

In truth, the coming together of elite and popular literature that Oprah's choice of The Corrections represented had many thinkers furrowing their brows even before the celebrated falling out. And, ironically, the economic ground that Bloom stood on to negotiate the abyss between high and low culture was the path Oprah walked to success with the Book Club. Americans, even the most elite, are notorious for not arguing with success. That's where Franzen miscalculated.

McLiterature

Yet Franzen's too-public reservations about the Book Club were only a restatement of comments I have heard students and professors making

for years. For those "in the high-art literary tradition," the oprahfication
of books was never just about the middlebrow status of the novels or the
confessional talk show slant to some of the literary discussions. Rather,
it was about the commodification of books, how Oprah transforms
books into consumer products, indistinguishable from microwaves or
DVD players.[16] The big issue, for many, was the sound of money in
Oprah's voice, to paraphrase Jay Gatsby, the clinking of coins every
time she announced a new novel.

Just as Gatsby's observation put Daisy in a harsh light, Oprah's en-
dorsement of *The Corrections*, some thought, tarnished Franzen's golden
image. Could the book possibly be good, they wondered confidentially,
if so many people like it, if it sells like McDonald's hamburgers? I have
observed that many arguments condemning Oprah's aesthetic choices
are, like this one, arguments on economic principle—and generally uninformed ones. Readers who trash Oprah Books usually can't name more
than one title. Literary prizewinners? Respected by other writers? You
would never know from the widespread assessment of the Book Club as
kitsch. Franzen must have feared being painted with that same brush.[17]

Yet, taken outside of the context of Oprah's marketing success,
many of the Oprah novels are, again, aesthetically excellent by academic standards, claiming unquestionable high art literary clout. That
doesn't matter when the novels enter the gaudy world of mass production, when they sit on the bestseller list next to *Chicken Soup for Dummies*.
Cultural theorists give context to this divide with their distinction between economic capital, how much money you have, and cultural capital, how "classy" you are. Rich people, most of us have noticed, aren't
always classy people. When they aren't, when they build garish man-
sions and fill them with velvet paintings, they have economic capital
and little cultural capital. On the other hand, when I look at my college
professor paycheck and realize that it is smaller than my older brother's
truck driver paycheck, I comfort myself, as I was subtly but carefully
taught to do in graduate school, that my job has cultural capital—not
more money but more social distinction.

The way these two types of capital separate themselves in the
United States is unique to us. We are, stereotypically, the world's obnox-
ious rich cousin, throwing back Cokes and hanging out at the mall in

$100 sneakers; we have money but no class. The French are our (irritat-ingly perfect) prototype of people with cultural capital but little eco-nomic capital, living in tiny apartments, eating gourmet food, and talking about art. American attitudes are also complicated by the democratic angel on our shoulder, whispering that if something is worth having, everyone should have a shot at it. If Starbucks coffee really is the best, why hoard it for an elite few in Seattle? Things really get murky when we take books that have cultural capital and try to get them out to more peo-ple, thus turning them into consumer products to be bought and sold.

As D. T. Max wrote in the *New York Times Magazine*, critics don't want to see a list like Oprah's that can't distinguish between "Edwidge Danticat, a delicate literary writer whose books sold modestly, and Maeve Binchy, a commercial writer whose perky *Tara Road* was already . . . [a] bestseller [before it became an Oprah Book]." Publishers, he says, "treat one as art and the other as commerce; *one gets prestige, the other money.* But within the world of Oprah, they are equals" [emphasis mine].[18]

Media accounts of the Franzen flap reflect this high cultural un-ease about the context that Oprah's Book Club creates. Yet, when the commentators sympathized with Franzen's reluctance to appear on *Oprah!* (why jeopardize high cultural capital?), no one stepped up to condone his kamikaze economic behavior. Instead, they asked how he could bite the hand that would feed him. How could he turn up his nose at the surest shot at financial success a contemporary writer has? And furthermore (maybe a bit halfheartedly), how dare he pretend that his work is too good to share with the masses?

I experienced a similar conflict when, in the midst of researching this book, I began to put the Book Club in the context of other Oprah shows. I tuned into a pre-Christmas program and found myself spun into an hour-long consumer frenzy. It was the much-anticipated, twice-yearly "O List" show, where Oprah gives away literally hundreds of dol-lars worth of free stuff to every guest in her audience. Pants, candles, shoes, electronics—you name it. If Oprah likes it, she's giving it away on this show. Stuff overflowed from the audience members' laps into piles of conspicuous consumption all over the studio. I watched open-mouthed, both appalled and envious. Was this incredibly tacky or un-believably generous? Did I want to run screaming from the room or do

my best to get on the next show? Both/and. It was as a moment of genuine American ambivalence.

Serious readers had been trying to resolve these conflicting values
since Oprah's Book Club became a phenomenon. As a culture, we were
placing increasing emphasis on literacy. Yet, when Oprah publicly
demonstrated the joys of reading and encouraged millions of people to
make time for good novels, why weren't serious readers, professors, and
teachers the first to jump on the Oprah bandwagon? Instead of "You go,
girl," we were saying, "I read that before Oprah chose it" and removing
the Oprah seal from our books.

Those of us who love reading like to think that books aren't just
stuff, and choosing good ones is fundamentally different from finding
the perfect pair of black pants. It's a deeper, more intellectual, even spiritual enterprise. On the other hand, we live in a world in which "a good
writer is a rich writer and a rich writer is a good writer," as *Harper's* Editor
Lewis Lapham put it.[19] We can't get past that paradox. On *Oprah!*, in a
certain light, the Book Club doesn't look a lot different from the "O
List." After watching that show, I observed the big book giveaway at the
end of Book Club shows with a little more cynicism.

The split loyalty Americans have when it comes to what we value
is rough on critics, who are expected to represent the interests of cultural rather than economic capital. But if they do their jobs well, if, for
example, they convince readers that *The Corrections* is a must-read, then
the formerly elite product with cultural capital becomes a must-have
consumer item, and the critics' reputations expand. Then we have to
wonder if the critics' recommendations were self-promoting, aimed at
increasing their own popularity and, thus, based on economic rather
than artistic standards.

For Americans, artistic standards come trailing shrouds of an aristocratic Western cultural tradition, where real art is supposed to be
underappreciated, reserved for a discriminating few. Real artists sacri-
fice for their art, living in industrial lofts and struggling to put food on
their tables (if they take time to think about food at all). In this tradition, our culture holds up the image of a pained and passionate Poe or
Salinger, even while most Americans would personally prefer to be
Madonna or Andy Warhol. We like our artists lonely and starving in

garrets. If they step out into the street in expensive suits, we begin to doubt their commitment.

Claiming Cultural Capital

Because Oprah's Book Club takes place on daytime TV and is aimed at women, it is easily assessed as low on cultural capital—it just ain't classy. Because we can't deny its high economic capital, its profitability, we figure it as gaudy or cheap. But, as D. T. Max said, the Book Club blurs the boundaries between cultural and economic capital, art and business. While Oprah is modeling rich reading publicly, she also models public reading richly.

And the "richly" part is essential. For most of the Book Club's regular meetings over its first six years, the smaller dinner groups were held in the studio lushly outfitted as a study specifically for those programs. The stage was complete with thick carpeting, huge armchairs, heavy wooden bookcases, and a globe. Out of respect for their surroundings, no one, not even the writers, wore denim (though leather pants were apparently acceptable), and the guests always looked as if they had just bellied up to the Estée Lauder makeover counter. Oprah presided, often in a cashmere sweater and flashing diamond earrings, offering toasts in crystal wineglasses.

Earlier Book Clubs were linked more closely to the dinner, and guests exclaimed over "seared yellow-tailed tuna roasted with pistachios and black peppercorns" or a perfect crème brulée as they commented on the novels.[20] The show gave up the food talk early on when it pared down its focus to the book at hand. On later Book Club programs the camera would simply pan the dinner table briefly before settling in on the guests who had retired to the study area. But this link with fine food is significant in situating the work the Book Club does. It blurs traditional class distinctions, placing Oprah's middlebrow novels (and their readers) in the realm of high culture, thus making high culture accessible. You, too, can live like this, the Book Club declares. Not vicariously through the afternoon soaps. Not sometime in the future after you achieve financial security. But here and now. By reading.

Reading Morrison's books, remember, "is like savoring a gourmet dining experience. This is not like a fast-food read," Oprah said.[21] So ignore the Boston Market and McDonald's commercials at the station
break, and pick up this book.

For me, the book is always the fascinating factor. Again, the middlebrow novel has complicated status categories since those sentimental
novels and Book-of-the-Month Club books helped to construct us as
middle-class Americans. When, in the early twentieth century, professors started to teach American literature and to bring novels more com-
monly into their courses of study, they had to configure them as high
status, as worthy of attention at elite institutions where professors are
paid to reproduce cultural capital. So they brought the tools of textual
analysis from classical texts in Latin or Greek and from poetry, essays,
and scripture.

For American novels, the price of admission into this reflective
realm of legitimate literature was that they, too, would need to be sifted
and selected, the best elevated and the worst condemned. The standards
were ready and waiting, and throughout the early part of the twentieth
century these standards were increasingly hostile to the social aspects of
novels. So novels became lowbrow or highbrow, bad or good by way of
traditional standards of aesthetic merit that, again, were aristocratic in
origin and assumed the mediation of a discriminating few. Thus, the
early days of the twentieth century were a good time for Herman
Melville, for philosophical musings and dense poetic language that sold
poorly, and a bad time for Harriet Beecher Stowe, for social engagement
and uncomplicated narrative that sold phenomenally well. Poor Harriet
was so economically successful that she never made it to college until
the feminist critics brought her with them in the 1970s.

But the novel proved much more unruly and harder to control than
the (by then) carefully tamed classical texts. Applying aesthetic standards to constantly proliferating consumer products was challenging,
especially with that abominable middlebrow novel muddying the waters
between the good and the bad. Bestseller lists, established at the turn of
the twentieth century, manifest this challenge, as Michael Korda observes in *Making the List, A Cultural History of the American Bestseller 1900–1999*.
"From day one," he writes, the list "has always represented a reliable mix-

ture of the good and the bad, of quality and trash, of literature for the ages and self-improvement schemes that now seem merely weird to the extent they're remembered at all."[22]

And because most people insisted on reading without the proper training, they consistently elevated the bad over the good. Korda explains:

> From the very beginning, serious reviewers were dismayed with the bestseller list, and the marked tendency it demonstrated of Americans failing to heed the advice and warnings of book reviewers (then as now). Even today, a reader of the *New York Times Book Review* can hardly fail to note the obvious difference between the books that are prominently and/or seriously reviewed, and those that appear on the list, and there was certainly an initial reluctance, undiminished by time, to "rank" books by their sales, instead of by their merit.[23]

The task for the cultural aristocracy was to find a way to guide the novel-reading masses to come around to the elite's definition of "good." Again, the Book-of-the-Month Club is a helpful illustration of how American culture met this challenge.

Learning to Read

The Book-of-the-Month Club had an image problem similar to Oprah's, because the more popular it became—the more its economic capital accumulated—the more its cultural capital diminished. High culture critics began to assail it, as Janice Radway explains in *A Feeling for Books*, by arguing that the elite ought to be *naturally* elite, not institutionalized by clubs and lists. The argument was that "one did not need literary authorities [i.e., the Book-of-the-Month-Club Board of Editors] to identify the best because the best books would reveal themselves to individuals who exercised their individual faculties appropriately."[24] The critics of the Book-of-the-Month Club began to draw a line "between the individual, independent reader capable of actively seeking out real literature and an undifferentiated mass of passive consumers" or "the infantalized, passive dupes of the book clubs who were content with the hand-me-down opinions of eminent book jurors," Radway writes. (This will sound familiar to Oprah's Book Club readers.) The "intelligent minority," they argued, didn't need book clubs. They would choose the best by long-standing, reliable aesthetic standards. The cream would rise to the top, and these autonomous readers would naturally recognize and enjoy it.

Those independent individuals were, of course, hardly self-regulating. Ideally, they would have been carefully taught the reliable aesthetic standards by the proper authorities, and they would apply them just as they had been taught, just as the authorities dictated. As Radway concludes, "It seems evident that what really disturbed the critics of the books clubs was not so much the mob, but the prospect that the mob might now be led by the wrong cultural authorities."[25] The connection to the proper cultural authorities is simple to trace in the choices of the intelligent minority. If you wanted to be among that elite group, you would never admit that you found Joyce's *Ulysses* unintelligible, for example, or that you enjoyed Pearl Buck more than William Faulkner. Yet this emphasis on a false individuality remained throughout the twentieth century.

Harold Bloom is a case in point. As we have seen, he argues in *How to Read and Why* that ideal readers are solitary, not social. He compares his solitary readers to Herman Melville's Ahab, who is "American through and through . . . but always strangely free, probably because no American truly feels free unless he or she is inwardly alone."[26] With this lonely American in mind, Bloom addresses his book to "unfinished" readers, readers who are not yet "wholly [them]selves" and need someone to guide them through literature "in order to strengthen the self."[27]

But the lessons he offers are not suggestive lessons in principle but directive lessons in practice—here are the texts that solitary readers will devote their lives to reading (What to read and Who), and here is what they will find, if they read astutely. For example, he lectures readers who hesitate to embrace Jane Austen's directive Mr. Knightley for the hero that he is in the novel *Emma*:

There is no misandry in Jane Austen or George Eliot or Emily Dickinson. Elizabeth Bennet and Emma Woodhouse are not concerned either with upholding or undermining patriarchy. Being vastly intelligent persons . . . they do not think ideologically. To read their stories well, you need to acquire a touch of Austen's own wisdom, because she was as wise as Dr. Samuel Johnson. Like Johnson, though far more implicitly, Austen urges us to clear our mind of "cant." "Cant" in the Johnsonian sense, means platitudes, pious expressions, group-think. Austen has no use for it, and neither should we. Those who now read Austen "politically" are not reading her at all.[28]

What *Emma* is about, Bloom insists, is not any kind of social or political message—that women need meaningful work and suffer for the lack of it, for example. *Emma* is about the training of the main character's "undisciplined imagination." She must be rescued "through the agency of Mr. Knightley" to see that her imaginings are "mere delusions." When, with Knightley's guidance, she learns "to integrate wit and will" she becomes, for Bloom, "a splendid heroine." With Mr. Knightley by her side, and Mr. Bloom by ours, the right choices become much more obvious; he helps us to distinguish feminist cant from his Truth.

Like Bloom, Charles Van Doren and Mortimer Adler, authors of *How to Read a Book: A Classic Guide to Intelligent Reading* first published in 1940, aimed to make the lessons of college literature classes accessible to the general public. Their now-classic text has been through several editions and is still readily available in most bookstores. And it shares many of the assumptions of Bloom's book with a similar aim. They argue, revealingly, for example, that "to pass from understanding less to understanding more by your own intellectual effort in reading is something like pulling yourself up by your bootstraps."[29] But here are the esteemed professors ready to give you a hand with those darned bootstraps. To their credit, they don't offer the correct readings that Bloom does. In their brief chapters on "How to Read Imaginative Literature" and "Suggestions for Reading Stories, Plays, and Poems" they offer lessons in principle: "Don't try to resist the effect that a work of imaginative literature [meaning artistic works of fiction, mainly] has on you. Don't look for terms, propositions, and arguments in imaginative literature." But they end their book with a list of 137 great writers and their works that would be "worth your while" to read. The list, they admit, may sound familiar. Much of it comes from "two sets we ourselves have edited," *Great Books of the Western World* and *Gateway to the Great Books.*[30]

The List

This seemingly irresistible urge to list is another way of delivering standards of literary merit to the uninitiated. Making sure readers read the right things is a way to guide taste and one that has a history as a cottage industry in our capitalist economy. If upwardly mobile Americans were going to buy novels, why not offer them a lifetime's supply of the ones you recommend (and will make money selling and teaching), at the same time delivering up a little class to the masses? As French sociologist Pierre Bourdieu explains so convincingly in *Distinction*, his influential study of taste, our aesthetic choices are directly connected to our social background, yet we continue to divorce the social and the aesthetic and insist that taste is "a gift of nature," of sensitive spirit or high intellect. Think of the stock dramatic scene in which a working-class star experiences opera for the first time and can't hold back the tears. But careful observation makes evident that taste is, instead, a predictable product of upbringing and education. "Surveys establish that all cultural practices (museum visits, concert-going, reading, etc.), and preferences in literature, painting or music, are closely linked to educational level ... and social origin," Bourdieu writes.[31] That working-class star, in other words, is more likely to leave the opera at intermission and head across town to the NASCAR race.

What we choose to read, in other words, is a learned (and thus predictable) behavior. How we were taught to read influences our choices.[32] So when Adler and Van Doren tell us that "imaginative literature primarily pleases rather than teaches," they are indicating how imaginative literature ought to be read.[33] It is affective, they say; readers should pay attention to the multiple meanings of words, classify by genre, seek unity, and, finally:

> . . . we must remember the obvious fact that we do not agree or dis-
> agree with fiction. We either like it or we do not. Our critical judg-
> ment in the case of expository books concerns their *truth*, whereas
> in criticizing belles-lettres, as the word itself suggests, we consider
> chiefly their *beauty*. The beauty of any work of art is related to the
> pleasure it gives us when we know it well.[34]

To pay attention to the things Bloom, Van Doren, and Adler suggest, to
irony and solitude, to multiple layers of meaning, to the reader and author as co-conspirators, to the complexity of characters and the insights
they offer for self-understanding, steers us away from social messages.
Bloom is emphatic about this. "Western high culture" is in decline because "novels are overpraised for social purposes."[35] He reminds us repeatedly that novels are best when they transcend cultural and political
issues, when they enlighten a solitary individual. And thus he obscures
the novel's extroverted history, its tendency to engage the imagination
in social situations, to urge readers to connect experientially, not just
aesthetically through disembodied words or formal qualities.

In summary, if you want to elevate your taste, Adler and Van
Doren explain, you should read the way we tell you to. Then you will be
"competent to judge." When you find yourself *wanting* to read more of
the books we tell you to read, then you'll know you're there. And then
"you will probably find a large company of men and women of similar
taste to share your critical judgments. You may even discover, what we
think is true, that good taste in literature is acquired by anyone who
learns to read" [emphasis mine].[36]

This final lesson, while sounding democratic, functions in the opposite way. With strange roundabout logic, it invites readers to affirm
their possession of cultural capital by exercising it. As Douglas B. Holt,
a leading marketing theorist, explains, "whereas economic capital is expressed through consuming goods and activities of material scarcity and
imputed luxury, cultural capital is expressed through consuming via aesthetic and interactional styles that fit with cultural elite sensibilities and
that are socially scarce."[37] It's not so much what you buy as how you live,
what social choices you make. Those with high cultural capital will listen to NPR rather than the 1980s Rock station; they will live near

bookstores and ethnic restaurants not on one-acre plots at the end of cul-de-sacs. And, as they read their way down The List, they might find a few others who have read what they have read. They affirm each other's "independent" choices by striking up a conversation about the good book they have both read. And, in the end, Bloom's solitary readers are good readers only when they affirm their elite tastes socially, among the culturally approved choices. Thus, Holt continues, "status boundaries are reproduced simply through expressing one's tastes."[38]

In this way, the distinction between cultural and economic capital is maintained by relentlessly divorcing them from one another. Those with high cultural capital, reinforcing the social scarcity of their elite sensibilities, "tend to disavow mass culture even when mass-produced goods are of high quality, and they camouflage their use of mass-produced goods when using them is unavoidable," Holt explains.[39] So when Farrar, Strauss put the Oprah seal into the cover art of Franzen's *The Corrections*, it became a different book. It became a mass-produced, popular choice rather than a marker of distinction and taste. And elite readers began to insist on unmarked covers.

Reading for Class

But unmarked covers were a fine distinction, meaningful only to those few Americans who had, in Adler and Van Doren's sense, learned to read. What I encountered in my Fall 2001 section of the Oprah's Books course were students marvelously unaffected by Franzen's reputation, as were, I suspect, most Oprah readers. In October when they read the novel for class, most of them had heard of it only because it was an Oprah book (or because it was assigned), and they felt free to condemn it as "too long and boring." For emphasis (with a touch of high cultural clout), one woman added that she "would rather be at sea with Ishmael and Captain Ahab than read *The Corrections* again."[40]

As part of the final, my twenty-four students, first-years to seniors, traditional college age to retirement age and from various majors (though predominantly nursing and teaching), were required to describe their own standards of literary merit in the context of choosing one of the seven novels we had read as the best and one as the worst. More than half named Franzen's book the worst, twice as many as any other book. Among this half were some of the more experienced readers who appreciated Morrison's *The Bluest Eye* and Danticat's *Breathe, Eyes, Memory*. (Other assigned novels included *What Looks Like Crazy on an Ordinary Day*, *Deep End of the Ocean*, *She's Come Undone*, and *Open House*). Their comments on why Franzen's novel didn't work for them were revealing. While several noted that they had learned to appreciate it intellectually through the class discussion, they took it to task on empathic grounds. "I couldn't connect with any of the characters," was the most frequent comment. "I could not get emotionally involved in it," one woman observed. "I wasn't drawn in," said another.

On the other hand, the more popular of the Oprah books I teach are the ones that mix some literary sophistication with an invitation to connection—*White Oleander* or *She's Come Undone*, for example. In fact, many of my students condemn some Oprah novels, as Franzen did, for being too simple, overly emotional, or predictable. They want to be challenged intellectually and philosophically, much in the way my English majors learn to be challenged by texts, but also personally, epathically, and emotionally. They want the rich, multilevel readings that Oprah offered on her best Book Club shows.

My mostly middle-class St. Catherine's students, mainly educated for a profession in a curriculum heavy on the liberal arts, are, in my observation, fairly similar to Oprah readers and to what cultural critics call "the general reader." My experience as a teacher convinces me that most of them, even in today's busy reality TV world, want to love to read. They are looking for books that bowl them over, that draw them in, that are unforgettable. Books they can get lost in. And, like good twenty-first century citizens, they want to get to them right now, without having to go through stacks of mediocre stories on the way to that one great read. I suspect that is why students, friends, and acquaintances are always asking me for lists of good books. Traditionally, that's how we have done this—find trusted critics and have them give us titles. Here are the top twenty books every college student should know. These 100 are the best novels of the twentieth century. These beautiful leatherbound volumes feature the world's fifty greatest thinkers. These ten books, above all others, have stood the test of time. Variations on Adler and Van Doren's list abound wherever we look.

But as books are ever more readily available, as literacy rates rise and more of us invest in a college education, these old lists and their outworn standards are not enough. Indeed, I sometimes wonder how they survived for so long in a democratic nation. Sure, they simplify our choices, but what do they leave out? In a vast and diverse global information age like ours, the top 100 anything is no longer obvious. Top 100 for whom? And who says so? Everything around us has changed in the last thirty years in the United States, but The List and the elite standards that maintain it have stayed surprisingly the same. With the rise of social change movements like civil rights and feminism, readers like my students began demanding more connection to their lives, more relevance in their literature. And leading intellectuals, like Adler, Van Doren, and Bloom, kept saying, "See The List." The unspoken What and Who of Bloom's *How to Read and Why* are astonishing. No need to highlight those, his attitude states. They go without saying—Shakespeare, Henry James, Marcel Proust. "See The List."

Since the 1960s, the children of the Baby Boom have been flooding U.S. universities and colleges. After the influx of veterans on the WWII GI Bill came generous financial aid programs and growing state university and community college systems, as well as the establishment of merit-based (rather than class- or connection-based) admission at our most elite schools. Since mid-century, the face of higher education began to change. A second-generation eastern-European immigrant and a woman, I was one of those new faces. While the prototypical college-goers were in private schools preparing to get into the Ivy League or the Seven Sisters, checking off The List, reading Dante's *Inferno* and *The Scarlet Letter*, we were watching *Star Trek* reruns and reading Erich Segal. And with television blanketing the nation, mass culture was making a dent in everyone's psyche. It has become the prominent backdrop of our lives—not Homer but Homer Simpson. TV, and now the Internet.

To be successful, colleges had to take these new students and our different gifts seriously, to meet us where we were, not try to transform us into the privileged preppies we imitated but would never become. As a graduate literature student, I joined many grad students before me in challenging the centrality of Britain in our literary history, of white men, of New England. We asked to read books by writers from the working class, black writers, immigrants, southerners, women—writers who reflected the America we knew. Colleges responded by creating different kinds of English courses. Many schools even began to take TV and mass media seriously. And the traditionalists bewailed the decline of Western Culture. And then came Oprah.

Oprah understood what students have been saying for years but what many professors and arbiters of taste in our culture have failed to grasp—that today's world demands a different approach to books and to reading. If nothing else is apparent from a close reading of Oprah's Book Club, it is certainly clear that America doesn't read like it used to—though Bloom's *How to Read and Why* typifies the attempts of many professors to correct that. Despite these efforts, Americans aren't going to books seeking classical allusions and Shakespearean quotes as affirmations of our expensive education or cultural literacy, our superior understanding or elite sensibilities. Generally, though William Bennett assumes otherwise, we aren't looking for moral lessons or biblical references. We aren't even hoping for innovation and experimentation. The Modern Library tells us *Ulysses* is the greatest book of the twentieth century, but even though there are more college graduates among us, Americans are reading *The Pilot's Wife*—because Oprah suggested it. "What," gasps the critic of elite sensibilites, "is going on here?"

Among other things, contemporary criticism is going on. Reflecting the tenor of the times, many critics argue, as I have here, that reading is a social as well as solitary activity. We see reading not so much as the traditionalists do, as building a solid foundation for the preservation of culture and unexamined common values. For us it is as much about challenging and reconstructing (sometimes deconstructing) culture and values in the midst of momentous change. While reading still engages the solitary self in reflection and self-examination, for many readers, inspired by the absorbing worlds of novels, it is also about encountering diversity and making connections, even, put simply, starting conversations.

Oprah's Book Club demonstrates that this perspective is a more accurate reflection of where most reading Americans have gone. The Book Club invites readers to talk to each other over books, to share stories, to identify and empathize, to explore new life patterns, and even to change. By emphasizing the novel's talking life, Oprah affirms a democratic shift in what readers value in books.

Shifting Standards

Wendy Steiner, a noted literary scholar, reported a similar shift in literary values in an article for the *New York Times Book Review* in 1998, just as I was beginning this book. Steiner had just finished a study of contemporary American fiction for the *Cambridge History of American Literature*. In describing the work of more than ten years that went into this project, she traces a change in her thinking about what characterizes current fiction. "I assumed," she writes, "that the important fiction since the nineteen-fifties was post-*modern*—the esoteric, goofy, often elephantine work of Pynchon, Barth, Vonnegut, Coover and Hawkes." So, she decided early on to focus her study there, on the experimentalists. But going beyond the given wisdom of the critics and calling on the post-1960s scholarship, she added a chapter on women writers.

Completing her first draft in the late 1980s, Steiner recalls:

> Everyone believed [then] that women were still writing nine-teenth-century novels, or, at least that was what a lot of men, especially experimentalists, liked to say. John Barth used the label "premodern" for the works of [what he called] "most of our contemporary American women writers of fiction, whose main literary concern, for better or worse, [he said] remains the eloquent issuance of . . . secular news reports." I read a raft of women's novels—by Toni Morrison, Ursula K. LeGuin, Louise Erdrich, Alice Walker, Marilynne Robinson, Gloria Naylor—and they did seem different. They were rich in imagery and emotion, consumed by the desire to recover a lost or hidden past. They did not deny existential despair, but neither did they react to it with brittle intellectualism or irony. Instead of offering the blankness of Vonnegut's 'so it goes,' they dramatized their characters' suffering. I reported this supposedly premodern syndrome faithfully, without using the word "retrograde" except in quotes.[41]

But a funny thing happened on the way through revision, Steiner says. Contemporary fiction began to look more like her women writers than her experimentalists. A judge for the National Book Award, Steiner found that for her and many other critics "Authorial generosity and proportion seemed much more valuable than uncompromising irony . . . I yearned for fineness of touch—beauty—with the hunger of a starving person."

Then, Steiner observes, the literary prizewinners began to reflect this desire, with their lyricism and depth of feeling, their affirmation of hope in a context of irony. Then there seemed to be a more general "shift in taste toward a kind of fiction that was pioneered by contemporary women writers." She concludes that, "if the postmodern period opened with metafictional fireworks, it closes with the extraordinary commonplace of love."

What Steiner reports here is not only her own changing perception but a more wide-ranging shift in the way we're responding to contemporary fiction in the Age of Oprah. Now I'm not saying that the most popular things are the best. You couldn't pay me enough to watch an *American Pie* movie in any of its iterations, and I'll pass every time on a Danielle Steel or Nicholas Sparks novel. Just as I wouldn't argue that McDonald's hamburgers are the best food because more people buy them, I don't want to make the point that capitalism should guide matters of taste. However, I think we have moved beyond the opposing ridiculous point, that popularity (or femininity) inevitably breeds mediocrity. Again, more Americans are going to college, taking literature classes, joining book clubs, visiting bookstores, and thinking and talking about fiction. They may not know Literature-with-a-capital-L, but they know what they like. And what they like may not always be all that bad.

I'm just Jeffersonian enough to believe that the literary tastes that my students and Oprah's readers model are often valuable and informed, and that I can learn something in conversation with them. I am also aware that my role as a professor is to offer them what I have, the skills for more intellectual, reflective reading that I worked as hard to hone as my ex-brother-in-law worked to become a master stonemason. That's what I bring to the conversations. So I approach my students with the skills that allow me to read and understand texts that have been defined as high cultural, but with desires similar to theirs—a desire for authorial generosity and proportion, "a driving desire to know, to connect, to communicate, and to share," as Radway describes it.[42] These are the things that motivate many contemporary readers.

My study of the Book Club has similarly clarified both my larger understanding of what contemporary U.S. culture embraces as a good book and what my personal preferences look like. Like many Oprah readers, my dream of a contemporary novel demands emotional as well as intellectual commitment. I want to dive into it wholeheartedly. The best novel would meet my expectations; it would engross me on many levels with complex characters, a layered plot and lovely language. Without talking down or over-explaining, it would trust me as a reader to get it. And it would challenge me on social issues, on my understanding of people and life, opening new views or values or reinforcing the ones that are central to me. Like many of my students, I don't care if a novel is negative or depressing. I just want it to engage me, to invite me, as Toni Morrison said, into its unique landscape.

Anticipatory Marketing

Though Oprah's staff repeatedly denies the existence of an overt standard of aesthetic merit ("She just picks what she likes"), the Book Club placed these shifting standards in the public eye and institutionalized them.[43] Working from the populist assumptions of a talk show host, Oprah mastered a mantra that Franzen, among others, never learned: Trust readers. This mantra probably springs from a commercial base— these readers are the people who made her rich after all—but it has translated into a broad affirmation of democratic values in a realm where such values are rarely seen, the realm of the aesthetic. While Franzen wondered publicly if serious literature could have a popular audience, Oprah assumed it did. Then she offered her readers good fiction, sometimes a *Tara Road* or a *Pilot's Wife* with a clear, chronological plot and a feisty character to identify with, and sometimes a more difficult novel, a Joyce Carol Oates, Jane Hamilton, or Edwidge Danticat, because she hoped they would like what she likes.

I know many readers found the more serious fiction tough going, but that didn't stop them from buying it in record numbers. By all accounts they seemed to be *reading* the Book Club novels as well, albeit sometimes only with Oprah's coaching. And, again, what delights me most is that they were also talking about books. Indeed, Oprah's genius may simply be that she captured the book club trend on its way up.

Journalist Malcolm Gladwell calls this "anticipatory marketing"— getting to the future first. In the paradigm he describes in "The Coolhunt," innovators come along first, followed by those who aren't innovators themselves but can spot innovation. When it came to book clubs, Oprah caught cool early. She was, as Gladwell says, an "early adopter," one of "the opinion leaders in the community, the respected, thoughtful people who watched and analyzed what those wild innovators were doing and then did it themselves."[44] So when readers began, in the early 1980s, to band together in book clubs, to negotiate their standards of literary merit publicly and use novels to make personal connections, Oprah was quick to follow.

On my own "coolhunt," I read through trendspotter Faith Popcorn's *EVEolution: The Eight Truths of Marketing to Women*, and it struck me that most of it could have been subtitled "as seen on Oprah." As an entrepreneur, Winfrey did everything right, and businesses who want to market to women are now taking pages from her playbook. For example, the Book Club institutionalized reading, making being a book group member a desirable way of "meeting people, building relationships, finding like-minded people," which is Popcorn's rule number one. Don't think pink, she says, "think link" (really). Other Popcorn truths, any one of which could account for the success of Oprah's Book Club, include the following: Women have busy lives and need you to bring products directly to them; women are loyal and trust the brands their mothers and friends trust; and women think holistically—they want products that make them feel like better people.[45]

Bringing books into American women's living rooms was a good way to get women to embrace them. But a more significant innovation, in my estimation, was placing those books in a different context from other public book talk. On Oprah's Book Club, the author's voice was never the only voice and often not even the strongest one. Rather than interview an author as the authority sharing banter with the urbane intellectual interviewer, Oprah surrounded authors with everyday readers and staged a conversation—eventually an extended conversation, not just a quick segment at the end of a program devoted to other topics. On Oprah's Book Club, millions of Americans could listen to what cultural critics call "the general reader," just as they had been listening to "real people" since Phil Donohue altered the talk show format in the 1970s.[46]

It is true that like Bloom, Adler, and Van Doren, Oprah has a list, but it is certainly a much different sort of list, perhaps centrally because she begins from different questions, what might be called consumer-driven (I prefer democratic) questions. These questions start from the bottom, with her readers, rather than with a top-down assertion of aesthetic authority. I learned early as a teacher that "Did you like it?" yields responses distinct from "Was it good?" and leads to different literary values. Oprah is looking for books her readers will like, responding to their desire for stories, for strong characters, for connection.

Since I began this study, it has impressed me as a teacher that she used her influence to meet her women readers where they were. She didn't embark on a campaign to have them read what was good for them—a Jane Austen novel or a bit of Virginia Woolf (as I might).[47] Even her move into classics led first to Steinbeck, a solidly middlebrow and thoroughly reader-friendly writer. She took the books many of her readers usually read and went "one click up," as a character in *Midwives* says. And, more importantly, she modeled how to read these more challenging books in the context of a community of engaged readers. In this way, she rode the wave of the book club movement but also reinforced it by bringing its methods into the living rooms and minds of her millions of viewers.

Franzen, too, had hoped to bring more serious fiction to "the American mainstream," as he wrote in his April 1996 cover article for *Harper's Magazine*. Franzen, then at work on *The Corrections*, wrote in this essay of both his fear that "there was something wrong with the whole model of the novel as a form of 'cultural engagement'" and of his dream that he was wrong.[48] In this time just before Oprah's Book Club began, he lamented how little novels mattered to most Americans and how seldom good ones were read with the seriousness they deserved. "The institution of writing and reading serious novels is like a grand old Middle American city gutted and drained by superhighways," he wrote:

> Ringing the depressed inner city of serious work are prosperous clonal suburbs of mass entertainments: techno and legal thrillers, novels of sex and vampires, of murder and mysticism. The last fifty years have seen a lot of white male flight to the suburbs and to the coastal power centers of television, journalism, and film. What remains, mostly, are ethnic and cultural enclaves. Much of contemporary fiction's vitality now resides in the black, Hispanic, Asian, Native American, gay, and women's communities, which have moved into the structures left behind by the departing straight white male.[49]

Little wonder that despite his yearning for novels to matter, Franzen couldn't see when they did, because a lively, inventive cultural center looked like a gutted inner city to his shortsighted gaze. When it came down to it, he was shocked, shocked that his (realistic, social) novel would be placed next to some (realistic, social) Oprah books that were not as serious. Like most high cultural critics, he was blind to changes in reading habits led by the middle or lower classes, by people of color or women, blind to the value of anything that looked like mass market culture. If only he could have let the ladies of the Book Club have at it, he might have been surprised to see, even from his high cultural perch, how comfortably serious novels have always fit in with a little bonding and a friendly hug or two. Sometimes the pages don't even get bent.[50]

Oprah's Book Club was a phenomenal success because it recognized and embraced how most Americans read and value literature. Oprah's unique position in popular culture and, yes, capitalism allowed her to answer the call to give books a public forum, to place them in social contexts, and to take advantage of their power to connect us. The Book Club latched onto a book club movement already gathering strength, especially among U.S. women, and took full advantage of its ties to a long-standing American tradition of novel reading for literacy and social mobility, a tradition that continues to appeal to deeply held democratic values.

Conclusion

The Triumph of Cultural Democracy

One of the most frequently cited movie moments of the twentieth century is when the Wizard of Oz commands us to "Pay no attention to the man behind the curtain." Something about that little man gets to us, as we watch him desperately pulling at the levers controlling the smoke and bluster, clinging to his last tokens of The Great and Powerful Oz. Too late. The curtain is drawn, the superhuman is humanized, and his power will never be the same. Remember how he tries to pull the curtain back and keep the machine running? Pathetic. Impossible.

The result, that Dorothy has to rely on her own power to get back to Kansas, the power she had all along, is a lesson that's both typically American and, as we have seen, classically Oprah. This is a story we tell over and over, watch again and again. "Click your heels three times." It does more than substantiate my belief in the significance of shoes (which, my friends would tell you, is profound). It affirms self-reliance and confirms the failure of the old systems. In that, it is the perfect myth for what came to be called the American Century.[1]

The American Century saw the precepts on which our nation was founded gain worldwide credence. Freedom and individuality, celebrated in American writing from *The Declaration of Independence* to Walt Whitman to the latest Country song, became, in the twentieth century, our givens. "Let the People Decide" is now a global governing standard, so much so, as social scientist Alan Wolfe asserts in his book *Moral Free-dom*, that "By century's end . . . no Western society could be considered a good society unless its political system was organized along demo-cratic lines." Wolfe argues that the widespread embracing of this right of the people to obtain and exercise *political* power set the stage for a new kind of democratic *moral* power, as well. Americans, he explains, ex-panded democratic political tenets into their private lives and claimed "moral freedom," the "freedom over the things that matter most," the freedom to make moral decisions as we choose.[2]

Though it is plainly the logical extension of the democratic prin-ciples Americans espouse, moral freedom, Wolfe asserts, is radical. "In-deed, the common position among most Western thinkers," he writes, "has been to argue the necessity for moral constraint as a precondition for freedom in all other aspects of life." In the past, these thinkers con-tended that for the sake of order or in service of a higher truth, we had to submit our individual wills to religious authority, scientific reasoning, nature, or law. Unlimited personal freedom was never an option—until the late twentieth century. After all, without some absolute truth, some restraining context, what could we ground our democratic choices on?

Wolfe's book is based on his interviews with "Americans from all walks of life about the conditions for leading good and virtuous lives." He found, not surprisingly, that our moral values have become idiosyn-cratic, contingent, and practical, rather than constant, given, or ab-solute. We have, in effect, pulled back the curtain on organized religion and Western philosophy. We haven't abandoned them. We visit them often like kindly old uncles for solid advice, but we follow our own paths when it comes to making choices.

David Brooks makes a similar argument in *Bobos in Paradise*, his 2000 book of "comic sociology" about the new bourgeois bohemian (bobo) values.[3] Observing educated, affluent Americans, he concludes that, since they began to leave old values behind in the 1950s, they have developed into "individualistic pluralists" who believe that "there cannot be one path to salvation. There are varieties of happiness, distinct moralities and different ways to virtue."[4] So Bobos make choices. They take new-age journeys and seek spirituality. And when, sometimes, they choose to be religiously observant, they practice "rigor without submission."[5] Even the most orthodox, he argues, pick and choose what they will believe—the way many observant Catholics in my college community enthusiastically support the church's social justice work but reject its condemnation of birth control, for example.

Lately, it seems most Americans don't grant absolute authority to anyone and are suspicious of those among us who do. In the sixty-plus years since we first met the wizard in the 1939 film, Americans have become postmodern.[6] We have rolled back the cameras to see the corporate suits behind the TV ads and the teleprompters informing Peter Jennings what to say next. And, more profoundly, we encountered Hitler, Stalin, and Osama bin Laden. Now we're not just notoriously antimonarchy like our eighteenth-century counterparts; at our best, we are also the ultimate antifascists. The more assertion of authority, from gods or men, the more suspicious we become. What right does anyone have, the typical American wants to know, to tell *me* what to think or do?

Is it any wonder, then, that Oprah has become the perfect guru for this democratic age? Much more like Glinda the Good Witch than the pompous wizard, she speaks softly in America's ear, reminding us that we know how powerful we are, that we control our own choices, that we don't need smoke and mirrors when we're already wearing the right shoes. Daytime TV viewers celebrate Oprah, because, like Glinda, she effectively affirms and reflects their values. Spiritual pluralism, moral freedom, and personal autonomy are staples on *Oprah!;* Oprah's experts regularly encourage guests and viewers to identify and exercise individual choice in relationships, parenting, health and fitness, spirituality, even shoe shopping.

So when Oprah started recommending novels, it seemed like a small step for Oprah viewers. In truth, it was a leap for literature, a leap into cultural democracy.

Cultural Democracy

Cultural democracy is founded on aesthetic freedom, the counterpart of Wolfe's moral freedom. Like moral freedom, it takes the political tenets of democracy into the personal realm and founds aesthetic value on individual choices rather than on absolute principles. Cultural democracy insists that there is no one standard of literary merit "delivered on tablets of bronze into the hands of T. S. Eliot," as a leading American literature critic famously said.[7] The cultural aristocracy has fallen, and, in matters of taste as in matters of politics and morality, we insist on democracy; we have become, as Brooks says, "individualistic pluralists." Now there are a variety of ways to judge what is good, and we want to use them all.

In general, Americans negotiate aesthetic freedom much as we do moral freedom, by finding tentative values that work for us, borrowing them from whatever cultural sources appeal. In his chapter on Bobo spirituality, for example, Brooks cites a woman who describes herself as a "Methodist Taoist Native American Quaker Russian Orthodox Buddhist Jew."[8] Likewise, an Oprah reader might pick up Adler and Van Doren's book, listen to what the members of her book group value, visit an online book discussion with the author, follow her own established preferences, pay attention to the questions posted on Oprah's website, and recall the lessons of her college literature class, all while reading the Book Club's latest selection. None of these sources serve as her final authority, and all of them can influence her decisions about a book's merit.

Oprah's novels also allow for this kind of sampling. In the context of the Book Club, novels can enlighten and entertain, aid self-improvement, or provide aesthetic pleasure. They highlight social justice issues and open avenues for compassionate connection—both within the texts and beyond them. They are, again, reflective, empathic, or inspirational, sometimes all three. Calling a novel "good" or even "great," as literary authorities have traditionally done, means very little until we can establish the context—for whom, in what situation, and according to which standards. In my experience, a book that is great for a literature class can be a flop in my book club. The criteria for excellence change with the circumstances.

This is where Oprah's method of using novels to invite social interaction as well as intellectual engagement and personal transformation affirms a wider and more generous standard for evaluating fiction, a standard that has always existed in the margins where readers loved and were moved by books, but that was seldom acknowledged in educated assessments of literature. In this age of book clubs, admiring good writing is no longer a leisure activity of the educated, the marker of prestige and privilege that other Americans aim for. Even academic high culture is recognizing that reading, valuing, and assessing literature is, and long has been, a democratic activity, one that everyone can engage in on whatever terms they like. And Oprah's Book Club is setting the tone. Recall the Book Club meeting on *The Bluest Eye*, where observations about character and language played side-by-side with messages of self-improvement and insights about racism and its effect on children.

Confronted with the variety of choices available in a cultural democracy, Oprah readers and book club members all over the country have responded with a yearning for talk. Wolfe, explaining moral freedom, writes:

> Our respondents are not saying . . . that in the absence of God, anything goes. They are instead expressing a desire to *have a conversation with* God, or with any other source of moral authority, in which they will not just listen, but be free to express their own views. [emphasis mine.][9]

Like the Americans Wolfe studied and the book group readers in Elizabeth Long's research, Oprah readers do not reject traditional aesthetic values, as we saw in the *Paradise* discussion. They do, however, reject their absolute authority. They approach them, instead, as one option among many.[10] They begin a conversation with them. Oprah readers' assessments aren't uninformed and value-free because their aesthetic is not the traditional one critics praise. Their aesthetic preferences seem to be, like the moral standards Wolfe observed, idiosyncratic, situational and practical, rather than constant, given, or absolute.

These standards, as I have seen them modeled on the Book Club, involve the readers' investment in and serious conversation with social issues, sometimes to the detriment but seldom to the exclusion of more traditional standards of aesthetic merit. In fact, it is hard to forget literature's elite roots when you're sitting in a studio that resembles the library of a Victorian men's club. But remember this is cultural democracy, where individualistic pluralists accumulate a variety of ways to judge what is good and try to use them all.

This version of aesthetic choice fits perfectly with the theory of relativism developed most famously for students of literature by Professor Barbara Herrnstein Smith.[11] This is not "radical relativism," which would be the opposite of absolute truth ("in the absence of God, anything goes"). It is contingent relativism, constructed not in the absence of truth, but in the context of many truths, negotiated truths, truths that people arrive at in conversation with others and with their own often-contradictory values. This version of aesthetic choice also makes the move from solitary to social reader overt. It requires that books have a talking life in order for readers to explore and work their way through the myriad of possible responses.

But as natural as the emphasis on conversation and on the social aspects of reading seems for Oprah readers, it is a seismic value shift for aesthetic theorists. As Pierre Bourdieu writes in his study of taste, "Detachment, disinterestedness, indifference—aesthetic theory has so often presented these as the only way to recognize the work of art for what it is, autonomous, *selbständig*, that one ends up forgetting that they really mean disinvestment, detachment, indifference, in other words, the refusal to invest oneself and take things seriously."[12] A traditional aesthetic of disinterested appreciation of beauty or form assumes a position of privilege where cultural and political issues can potentially be insignificant to everyday life; it assumes, in other words, an aristocratic audience. The postmodern aesthetic of cultural democracy gives us a way to bring literature into the everyday lives of diverse readers with various interests. It opens new ways to take books seriously and invest in them.

When book groups talk about what they value most in a novel, it's not surprising, then, that many of them come up with the same new coinage: "discussabilty."[13] Not complex language, not compelling plots, not even characters they can sympathize with. They want to read books that motivate engaging conservations, conservations that will make sense of their range of readings.

But to complete the reading revolution that Oprah's Book Club represents, this "discussability" must involve a more overt conversation about aesthetic values, otherwise the most widley taught traditional values will enter the conversation silently and uncontested or, worse, will be dismissed as irrelevant. Remember that first Book Club meeting when Oprah asked a reader of *Deep End of the Ocean*, "What did you like about it?" That's where our conversation began, and that is where I would direct it again, in conclusion. To revisit that question with the seriousness it deserves would solidify the important changes Oprah has begun to shape on the Book Club.

I think of a reader who Oprah quoted nearly as often as she cited Morrison's "That, my dear, is called reading"—the reader who insisted that she loved being a member of Oprah's Book Club, even though, as she told Oprah, "I don't actually read the books you pick." She picked her own books, she said, and read along with the Book Club.[14] Even as she insisted on her own choices, she still wanted to be in on the conversation. This woman made the important move from reader to self-reliant critic, a move that Oprah praised and encouraged again and again.

In retelling this woman's story, Oprah highlights how very differently she inhabits the role of list-maker and cultural arbiter of taste. Here she is not so much the authoritarian wizard, she-who-must-not-be-defied, as she is the encouraging Glinda, encouraging women to read because it will make their lives better. And, like Glinda, she recognizes that her readers already have the equipment they need to be readers and to make good choices. She doesn't direct them how to read; she puts them on stage and lets them model diverse, idiosyncratic reading practices themselves. But highlighting these reading practices and making overt the questions of taste would allow Oprah readers to be more thoughtful about their answers to the question "What did you like about it?"

White Oleander

A contrast of my students' classroom responses to *White Oleander* and those that were highlighted on the Book Club program is helpful here.[15] In both forums the readers discussed plot, setting, and characters and their personal connections to all three. In both, the focus was on "the way she writes," the carefully crafted language of Janet Fitch's novel. The Book Club reading, however, presented this as a fait accompli. Pulling comments from the audience to reinforce the point, Oprah introduced *White Oleander* as "one of my best picks ever." (Again, she added it to the short list of favorites on her website afterward.) "You see the world differently after you read it," she explained, because, she says, of the deeper sensitivity the language gives you, especially to the nuances of the natural world.

My students, on the other hand, made the language a central point of debate. They questioned its artistic value. The writing, some thought, was overwrought and self-consciously artistic, an observation reinforced by Fitch's explanation on the program that *any* descriptive phrase she had heard before she considered a cliché and avoided. One student cited, as an example, this confusing use of images and mixed metaphor from the novel: "smog lay thick over the Valley like a vast headache over a defeated terrain, obscuring the mountains." The students' careful observations and lively debate of the novel's aesthetic merit was a key difference from the Book Club discussion. In this context, even some students who liked the novel very well as a compelling story could also critique it carefully, as they named their preference for transparent language that doesn't call attention to its own literariness—and for a shorter, more precise unfolding of plot. I believe that this sort of critique is essential for readers to engage as they answer the question "What did you like about it," the question that must guide the self-reliant critic in her conversations about, and choice of, books.

The Oprah's Book Club meeting on *White Oleander* did feature a disagreement. But, like most Book Club disagreements, it was not about literary merit, a question that is seldom engaged, but about a social issue—the underage main character, Astrid, having sex with Uncle Ray, her foster father. Was it abuse or love, the dinner guests wondered—as did my students. It was a lively discussion in both forums, where disagreement was a catalyst for careful consideration. Disagreement, many book club members claim, is the hallmark of their discussions, the way they challenge each other's thinking.[16]

As the Book Club sets its sights on classics, I hope Oprah readers will be invited to debate the aesthetic as well as social aspects of the books, to analyze the cultural standards that make something classic as they explore their own preferences. A good book club, like a good literature class (and a good democracy), would embrace disagreement and dissent, let ideas confront each other openly, and encourage independent thinkers to evaluate the relative merit of these ideas in conversation.

Then, unlike Bloom and Adler and Van Doren's readers who know they have arrived when they stop asking Who to read and What, Oprah readers will effectively complete their American move toward cultural democracy when they *start* asking those exact questions, when they challenge given standards of taste in social contexts—even, like the reader who chooses her own selections, Oprah's context. Because books like *How to Read a Book* and *How to Read and Why* still assume a cultural aristocracy, a happy few who guide others around the monuments of Western Culture via a traditional aesthetic, they assume that the culture wars are going in their favor. They're wrong. We live in an age of moral relativism that parlays itself into an aesthetic relativism—in popular culture and even among those who dominate our corporate, political, and academic institutions. Warhol's tomato soup cans are just down the gallery from Vermeer; lovers of Tosca have offices next door to Smashmouth fans; the city orchestra plays Cole Porter one night and Bach the next. The monuments of Western culture are, for most Americans, a bit like the crumbling Ozymandias and his "vast and trunkless legs of stone" standing in the empty desert: "Look on my Works, ye Mighty, and despair!"[17]

Whether Ozymandias, Oz, or Oprah speaks, Americans will insist on being free to challenge their authority (sometimes even as they tremble and despair–or run out to buy the book). And just as they challenge authority in other areas of their lives, independent readers and self-reliant critics in a cultural demoracy should be free to challenge aesthetic authority as well.

After a century that claimed the rights of democracy, finally, for nearly all Americans by extending civil rights to African Americans and women, by opening the gates of colleges and universities, by legislating employment nondiscrimination, Oprah is shaping and advocating cultural democracy in her push to get America reading again. Using her TV talk show, she advances on Old World privilege and elitism with her guerilla force of women readers behind her. Refusing her own authority and highlighting everyday women's voices, she pushes the middlebrow novel forward, letting it complete the aesthetic coup it began in America more than 200 years ago, the triumph of the social life of literature. In the process, this TV talk show host is changing the way America reads. Now that's a story worth talking about.

Oprah's Book Club List
ALPHABETICAL, FIRST SIX YEARS

Title	Author	Announcement Date	Weeks on NYTimes Hardcover List	Weeks on NYTimes Paperback List	Sales figures (when available)
Back Roads	Tawni O'Dell	3/28/00	8	5	635,000 hardcover 2000
The Best Way to Play	Bill Cosby	12/8/97	20	7	529,104 hardcover 1998 / 1,000,000 paperback 1999
Black and Blue	Anna Quindlen	4/9/98	11	9	979,004 paperback 2000
The Bluest Eye	Toni Morrison	4/27/00		17	
The Book of Ruth	Jane Hamilton	11/18/96		6	458,600 paperback 1998
Breath, Eyes, Memory	Edwidge Danticat	5/22/98			
Cane River	Lalita Tademy	6/20/01	17		587,248 hardcover 2001 / 239,534 paperback 2002
The Corrections	Jonathan Franzen	9/24/01	9	5	930,000 hardcover 2001 / 447,776 paperback 2002
Daughter of Fortune	Isabelle Allende	2/17/00	8		562,672 hardcover 2000 / 380,781 paperback 2000
The Deep End of the Ocean	Jacquelyn Mitchard	9/17/96	29	16	840,263 hardcover 1996 / 1,904,414 paperback 1997
Drowning Ruth	Christina Schwarz	9/27/96	14	3	750,00 hardcover 2000 / 427,602 paperback 2001 / 148,542 2002
Ellen Foster	Kaye Gibbons	10/27/97		13	
Fall on Your Knees	Ann-Marie MacDonald	1/24/02		14	878,900 paperback 2002
A Fine Balance	Rohinton Mistry	11/30/01		6	542,725 paperback 2001
Gap Creek	Robert Morgan	1/18/00	13	1	638,000 hardcover 2000 / 380,000 paperback 2000 / 88,300 2001
The Heart of a Woman	Maya Angelou	5/9/97		25	600,000 paperback 1997
Here on Earth	Alice Hoffman	3/6/98		10	1,050,000 paperback 1998 / 950,000 1999

Title	Author	Date			Sales
House of Sand and Fog	Andre Dubus III	11/16/00		20	1,304,390 paperback 2000 / 717,073 2001
*I Know This Much Is True	Wally Lamb	6/18/98	19	8	756,051 hardcover 1998 / 884,316 paperback 1999
Icy Sparks	Gwyn Hyman Rubio	3/8/01		11	1,004,231 paperback 2001 / 112,000 2002
Jewel	Bret Lott	1/19/99		9	1,000,000 paperback 1999 / 975,000 2000
A Lesson Before Dying	Ernest Gaines	9/22/97		8	
A Map of the World	Jane Hamilton	12/3/99		14	501,570 paperback 2000
The Meanest Thing to Say	Bill Cosby	12/8/97			
Midwives	Chris Bohjalian	10/20/98		20	898,000 paperback 1998 / 443,692 1999 / 81,737 2001
Mother of Pearl	Melinda Haynes	6/15/99	13		592,625 hardcover 1999 / 350,000 paperback 2000
Open House	Elizabeth Berg	8/23/00	10		581,715 hardcover 2000 / 312,309 paperback 2001
Paradise	Toni Morrison	1/16/98	18		804,862 hardcover 1998
The Pilot's Wife	Anita Shreve	3/31/99		28	2,279,134 paperback 1999 / 530,629 2000
The Poisonwood Bible	Barbara Kingsolver	6/23/00	(29)	43	(300,000+ hardcover 1998) / (662,842 paperback 1999) / 1,759,929 2000 / 450,000 2001
The Rapture of Canaan	Sheri Reynolds	4/8/97		8	1,000,000 paperback 1997
The Reader	Bernhard Schlink	2/26/99		15	1,528,615 paperback 1999
River, Cross My Heart	Breena Clarke	10/14/99		7	770,889 paperback 1999
She's Come Undone	Wally Lamb	1/22/97		35	1,520,556 paperback 1997 / 1,200,000 1998 / 100,000+ 1999
Song of Solomon	Toni Morrison	11/18/96		16	

(continued)

Title	Author	Announcement Date	Weeks on NYTimes Hardcover List	Weeks on NYTimes Paperback List	Sales figures (when available)
Songs in Ordinary Time	Marry McGarry Morris	6/18/97		16	1,120,000 paperback 1997
*Stolen Lives: Twenty Years in a Desert Jail	Malika Oufkir	5/16/01	19	4	477,867 hardcover 2001
Stones from the River	Ursula Hegi	2/28/97		21	1,285,000 paperback 1997
Sula	Toni Morrison	4/5/02		1	720,000 paperback 2002
*Tara Road	Maeve Binchy	9/4/99		8	950,000 hardcover 1999 / 1,026,000 paperback 2000
The Treasure Hunt	Bill Cosby	12/8/97			
Vinegar Hill	A. Manette Ansay	11/10/99		8	
A Virtuous Woman	Kaye Gibbons	10/27/97		11	
We Were The Mulvaneys	Joyce Carol Oates	1/24/01		16	1,550,000 paperback 2001 / 180,000 paperback 2002
What Looks Like Crazy on an Ordinary Day	Pearl Cleage	9/25/98		8	743,318 paperback 1998
Where the Heart Is	Billie Letts	12/7/98		30	770,561 paperback 1998 / 1,224,745 1999 / 184,951 2001
While I Was Gone	Sue Miller	5/26/00		16	1,313,170 paperback 2000 / 187,384 2001
*White Oleander	Janet Fitch	5/6/99	18	14	903,729 hardcover 1999 / 620,094 paperback 2000 / 114,259 2001 / 592,895 2002

* = Chosen while available only in hardcover

( ) = Numbers before selection as an Oprah book

Sales figures come from *Publishers Weekly* year-end reports by Daisy Maryles as printed in the *Bowker Annual* (see note to page 4), and are based on shipped and billed figures supplied by publishers of new books. They should not be considered final net sales.

Oprah's Book Club List
CHRONOLOGICAL—FIRST SIX YEARS

2002 _____

Sula
by Toni Morrison
Announced April 5, 2002
New York: Penguin, 1973

Fall on Your Knees
by Ann-Marie MacDonald
Announced January 24, 2002
New York: Scribner, 1996

2001 _____

A Fine Balance
by Rohinton Mistry
Announced November 30, 2001
New York: Vintage, 1995

The Corrections
by Jonathan Franzen
Announced September 24, 2001
New York: Farrar, Straus and Giroux, 2001

Cane River
by Lalita Tademy
Announced June 20, 2001
New York: Warner, 2001

Stolen Lives: Twenty Years in a Desert Jail
by Malika Oufkir
Announced May 16, 2001
New York: Hyperion, 1999

Icy Sparks
by Gwyn Hyman Rubio
Announced March 8, 2001
New York: Penguin, 1998

We Were the Mulvaneys
by Joyce Carol Oates
Announced January 24, 2001
New York: Plume, 1997

2000

House of Sand and Fog
by Andre Dubus III
Announced on November 16, 2000
New York: Vintage, 1999

Drowning Ruth
by Christina Schwarz
Announced on September 27, 2000
New York: Doubleday, 2000

Open House
by Elizabeth Berg
Announced on August 23, 2000
New York: Random House, 2000

The Poisonwood Bible
by Barbara Kingsolver
Announced on June 23, 2000
New York: HarperCollins, 1998

While I Was Gone
by Sue Miller
Announced on May 26, 2000
New York: Ballantine, 2000

The Bluest Eye
by Toni Morrison
Announced on April 27, 2000
New York: Simon and Schuster, 1970

Back Reads
by Tawni O'Dell
announced on March 28, 2000
New York: Viking, 2000

Daughter of Fortune
by Isabelle Allende
announced on February 17, 2000
New York: HarperCollins, 1999

Gap Creek
by Robert Morga
Announced on January 18, 2000
Chapel Hill, NC: Algonquin, 1999

1999 _____

A Map of the World
by Jane Hamilton
Announced on December 3, 1999
New York: Doubleday, 1994

Vinegar Hill
by A. Manette Ansay
Announced on November 10, 1999
New York: Avon, 1994

River, Cross My Heart
by Breena Clarke
Announced on October 14, 1999
Boston: Little, Brown, 1999

Tara Road
by Maeve Binchy
Announced on September 4, 1999
New York: Delacorte, 1998

Mother of Pearl
by Melinda Haynes
Announced June 15, 1999
New York: Hyperion, 1999

White Oleander
by Janet Fitch
Announced on May 6, 1999
Boston: Little, Brown, 1999

The Pilot's Wife
by Anita Shreve
Announced on March 31, 1999
Boston: Little, Brown, 1998

The Reader
by Bernhard Schlink
Announced on February 26, 1999
New York: Vintage, 1997

Jewel
by Bret Lott
Announced on January 19, 1999
New York: Simon and Schuster, 1991

1998

Where the Heart Is
by Billie Letts
Announced on December 7,1998
New York: Warner, 1995

Midwives
by Chris Bohjalian
Announced on October 20, 1998
New York: Random House, 1997

What Looks Like Crazy on an Ordinary Day
by Pearl Cleage
Announced on September 25, 1998
New York: Avon, 1997

I Know This Much Is True
by Wally Lamb
Announced on June 18, 1998
New York: HarperCollins, 1998

Breath, Eyes, Memory
by Edwidge Danticat
Announced on May 22, 1998
New York: Random House, 1994

Black and Blue
by Anna Quindlen
Announced on April 9, 1998
New York: Dell, 1998

Here on Earth
by Alice Hoffman
Announced on March 6, 1998
New York: Berkley, 1997

Paradise
by Toni Morrison
Announced on January 16, 1998
New York: Knopf, 1998

1997 _____

The Meanest Thing to Say
by Bill Cosby
Announced on December 8, 1997
New York: Scholastic, 1997

The Treasure Hunt
by Bill Cosby
Announced on December 8, 1997
New York: Scholastic, 1997

The Best Way to Play
by Bill Cosby
Announced on December 8, 1997
New York: Scholastic, 1997

Ellen Foster
by Kaye Gibbons
Announced on October 27, 1997
New York: Vintage, 1987

A Virtuous Woman
by Kaye Gibbons
Announced on October 27, 1997
New York: Vintage, 1990

A Lesson Before Dying
by Ernest Gaines
Announced on September 22, 1997
New York: Vintage, 1994

Songs In Ordinary Time
by Marry McGarry Morris
Announced on June 18,1997
New York: Penguin, 1995

The Heart of a Woman
by Maya Angelou
Announced on May 9, 1997
New York: Random House, 1981

The Rapture of Canaan
by Sheri Reynolds
Announced on April 8, 1997
New York: Berkley, 1995

Stones from the River
by Ursula Hegi
Announced on February 28, 1997
New York: Scribner, 1994

She's Come Undone
by Wally Lamb
Announced on January 22, 1997
New York: Simon and Schuster, 1992

1996 _____

The Book of Ruth
by Jane Hamilton
Announced on November 18, 1996
New York: Doubleday, 1988

Song of Solomon
by Toni Morrison
Announced on November 18, 1996
New York: Penguin, 1977

The Deep End of the Ocean
by Jacquelyn Mitchard
Announced on September 17, 1996
New York: Penguin, 1996

Notes

Introduction

1. It is difficult for someone schooled in feminism and Associated Press journalistic style to refer to a woman by her first name. However, in this case, where "Oprah" is a household name, it seems absurd to refer to the star as "Winfrey." So I bow to popular culture and most often call her Oprah throughout the text. When I do make a distinction, I tend to make it between the TV show *Oprah!*, the TV icon "Oprah," and the thinking, reading person, "Winfrey."

2. Though I watched and recorded many of the Oprah Book Club shows beginning in 1998, I also use written transcripts of the shows throughout this text (video copies of earlier shows are unavailable according to Harpo, Inc., but tapes can be ordered for some shows aired the last two years of the Book Club). These official tapes and transcripts are available through Burrelle's Transcripts, P.O Box 7, Livingston NJ, 07039-0007, or at www.burrelles.com/transcripts. The announcement of the end of the Book Club came on the Book Club show that aired April 5, 2002.

3. The idea a book's "talking life," the encounter of the written word with the spoken, is central to this study, and is inspired by Toni Morrison's comment on the Book Club show about *Paradise* (transcript entitled "Book Club—Toni Morrison," March 6, 1998), cited in the epigraph to this text. The idea of "the talking book," however, is prominent throughout African American literary criticism, beginning, I believe, with Henry Louis Gates Jr.'s *The Signifying Monkey* (Oxford, 1988). See chapter two for a more complete discussion of this influence on Oprah's Book Club. Irene Kacandes also explored the idea of "talk reading" in her book *Talk Fiction: Literature and the Talk*

Explosion, which mainly explores talking or "secondary orality" as a quality of fiction rather than an orientation toward texts, as I use it. See note 46, ch. 4.

4. Throughout this text I use statistics compiled from my study of the *New York Times* "Bestseller Lists" (1994–2002), printed weekly in the *New York Times Book Review* and available online through FirstSearch. Averages are taken from my calculations based on information available in the *New York Times* bestseller lists and the *Publishers Weekly* year-end reports through 2002. See chart in Appendix A.

5. My understanding of the new format and Oprah's plans for it come from a conversation with a spokesperson for Harpo, Inc. on June 17, 2003, the day before Oprah announced her choice for the return of the Book Club. She explained that Oprah suspended the Book Club in April 2002 because she felt, at the time, that it was interfering with her enjoyment of reading. "The Book Club became more of an obligation than a pleasurable pastime," the spokesperson said. But when Oprah read a couple of books over the summer that she wanted to share, she decided to bring the Book Club back and focus on "great books that have stood the test of time"—not necessarily classics, she explained, not necessarily old books and not necessarily dead authors, but "great books."

6. Information on the makeup of Oprah's audience varies, but I pull this information from several studies of Oprah and of the *Oprah Winfrey Show* (see Brooks, Cloud, Epstein and Steinberg, Haag, Lowe, Masciarotte, and Squire) as well as on my own observation and questioning of Oprah viewers beginning in 1998. The numbers on viewership are culled from these sources, as well as an article in the *New York Times Magazine*, "The Oprah Effect" by D. T. Max (December 26, 1999, pp. 36–41).

7. "The usual sources" for English professors include the Modern Language Association Bibliography of articles and books in literature and languages, available on CD-ROM at most libraries, as well as "Expanded Academic ASAP," an online resource to article published in academic and related journals. I also mention other search tools—Lexis/Nexis, InfoTrac and FirstSearch, also online and available at most libraries.

8. My numbers on total sales of novels come from *Publishers Weekly* year-end reports by Daisy Maryles as printed in the *Bowker Annual: Library and Book Trade Almanac, Facts, Figures and Reports*, Dave Bogart, editor (New Providence, NJ: RR Bowker). For this and other reference help, I am indebted to St. Kate's incomparable Jim Newsome, our reference librarian for literary research, and to Jenn Jacobs, my research assistant and librarian-to-be.

Chapter One _____

1. The bookstore the three women walk into is the Midway Borders in St. Paul, my favorite public space for writing and thinking about Oprah's Book Club.

2. *Jet*, November 24, 1997, cover story and interview with Winfrey.

3. Winfrey's comments on reading come from Bridget Kinsella's article "The Oprah Effect" in *Publishers Weekly*, January 20, 1997 (v244 n3, p.276).

4. These numbers on *Deep End of the Ocean* are from an article by Paul Gray, "Winfrey's Winners," in *Time*, December 2, 1996 (v148 n25, p. 84).

5. In an interview with a spokeperson from Harpo, Inc. (who requested that I not include her name) in June 2002, I learned that audience members for the Book Club shows are instructed when they order their tickets to prepare for the show by reading the novel. If they don't want to, they are offered tickets to another show. It is a policy of the *Oprah!* show to have informed audience members, she explained. If a movie actor is the guest of the day, the audience will all screen his or her latest film before the show, for example, and they are always encouraged to read whatever book is featured, including self-help books, biographies, or Mattie Stepanek's poetry.

6. Again, quotations from the show come from my own recordings and written transcripts available through Burrelle's Transcripts, P.O Box 7, Livingston, NJ, 07039-0007, or at www.burrelles.com/transcripts.

7. Transcript entitled "Pregnant Women Who Use Drugs and Alcohol," September 17, 1996.

8. The philosophy professor here is Bernie Freydberg, who taught (played jazz and headed the boxing club) at Slippery Rock State College when I was a student there, 1979–1982. "The hairy professor" taught me logic, encouraged my journalism, and led me to Morrison and (like Jan Radway) the Book-of-the-Month Club version of the *Oxford English Dictionary*. (See chapter two for a discussion of BOMC, informed by Professor's Radway's influential work, *A Feeling for Books*.) He was also an early example to me of a traditional scholar—a classicist, in fact—who was engaged in contemporary art and social issues, whose intellectualism ranged widely and encompassed working-class and popular culture. He was, then, the perfect guide to Toni Morrison.

9. Transcript entitled "Newborn Quintuplets Come Home," October 18, 1996.

10. *Both House of Sand and Fog* and *The Corrections* were finalists for National Book Awards (*Corrections*, of course, won that award in 2001); *Fall on Your Knees* won the Commonwealth Writers Prize, as did *A Fine Balance. A Fine Balance* was also a finalist for the Booker Prize and won Canada's Giller Prize. *The Book of Ruth* is a Pen/Hemingway Awardee. Morrison has won nearly every literary prize available for her novels, including a 1978 National Book Critics Circle Award for *Song of Solomon* and a Nobel Prize (which cited *Beloved*). *A Lesson Before Dying* also earned a National Book Critics Circle Award in 1993. Others were *New York Times Book Review* notable books of the year, including *We Were the Mulvaneys, The Reader,* and *Poisonwood Bible. Map of the World* was named one of the ten best books of the year by *Publishers Weekly* and the *Miami Herald,* among others.

11. The idea that Oprah's books outclass their company is taken from a cover article in *Life* magazine (September 1997) by Marilyn Johnson and Dana Fineman, "Oprah Winfrey: A Life in Books."

12. Various writers used "the Oprah Effect" frequently in the online version of *Publishers Weekly*.

13. Sales numbers for *Song of Solomon* come from an article in *People Weekly* by Lan N. Nguyen (December 2, 1996, v46, n23, p. 36, web2.infotrac.gale-group.com/itw).

14. I sometimes use the averages from the first four years of the Book Club because that is when it met most regularly, becoming more random and less regular over the last year and a half. Averages for all Oprah Books are 17 weeks on the bestseller list and 1.2 million average yearly sales (see chart in Appendix A). Also, for the purpose of clarity, I count the two short Kaye Gibbons novels (*A Virtuous Woman* and *Ellen Foster*) as one selection because they were announced and discussed together. Wally Lamb's two novels and Jane Hamilton's are discussed separately because they were discussed on separate programs, a year or two apart. This is where my count differs (from their 46 to my 45) from those used by *Publishers Weekly* and Amazon.com (Oprah sometimes says 46 and other times 48). I also count all three children's books by Bill Cosby as one selection, the "Little Bill" books. These averages were last calculated in June 2003.

15. *East of Eden* numbers are from *Publishers Weekly* Newswire, June 20, 2003. Yearly sales of *Grapes of Wrath*, the editors note, are about 150,000, much of that attributable to students. *East of Eden* is generally Steinbeck's third most popular text.

16. My numbers on total yearly sales of novels come, again, from *Publishers Weekly* year-end reports by Daisy Maryles as printed in the *Bowker Annual: Library and Book Trade Almanac, Facts, Figures and Reports*, Dave Bogart, editor (New Providence, NJ: RR Bowker). I also pulled information from daily updates on the *Publishers Weekly* online newsletter (see note 23, ch. 1).

17. Maryles quote from the 1996 *Publishers Weekly* year-end tally, Bowker, p. 591.

18. "Touched by an Oprah" by Paula Chin and Christina Cheakalos (*People Magazine* 52:24 [December 20, 1999] pp. 112–122).

19. From a telephone interview with Elizabeth Berg, October 2000.

20. Maryles quote from the 1999 year-end *Publishers Weekly* tally, Bowker, p. 625.

21. D. T. Max's article for the *New York Times Magazine* (December 26, 1999, pp. 36–41) is a helpful look inside the workings of the Book Club, despite its sometimes condescending attitude. His insights were affirmed for me in an interview with a spokesperson for Oprah on July 11, 2002. She described a similar selection process, with many books being vetted, but with Oprah always reading and making the final choices herself.

22. Maryles quote from the 1997 year-end *Publishers Weekly* tally, Bowker, p. 621.

23. The average for all Oprah Books of 1.2 million copies came from my calculations of collected data, mainly from *Publishers Weekly*, but was confirmed by a *Publishers Weekly* report Tuesday April 9, 2002, shortly after Oprah announced the end of the Book Club. In that report, the editors listed the average sales of Oprah books by years as follows: 1996–1997, 1.3 million; 1998, 1.1 million; 1999, 1.5 million; 2000, 1.3 million; 2001, 700,000. The editors noted that the Book Club had slowed down during the last two years, meeting less regularly, which probably accounted for the drop in sales.

24. This list of recurring topics of the Book Club and its novels is taken largely from research done by students in my Oprah Books class at the College of St. Catherine, summer 2000. See the Acknowledgments for a list of their names. These students and the diverse students in my first Oprah Books class, summer 1999, from Japan, Malaysia, Russia, and France as well as the United States, were invaluable contributors to this project with their insights, observations, and enthusiasm.

25. Showalter's speculation about who buys novels is cited in a *New York Times* article by Bruce Weber entitled "When the I's of a Novel Cross Over" (February 6, 1999), B7. Showalter, author of *A Literature of Their Own*, was a leader from the beginning in the move to take women readers and writers seriously.

26. The "emperor's new book" is Bill Goldstein's coinage, from an article, "Let Us Now Praise Books Well Sold, Well Loved, But Seldom Read," in the *New York Times* (July 15, 2000, p. B11).

27. Since I teach American literature with particular attention to the American novel, I have trouble tracing where all my information comes from, culled as is from years of research and lectures. But information about the history of novels in the United States is most readily accessible from two articles I use often: Jane Tomkins's "Sentimental Power: *Uncle Tom's Cabin* and the Politics of Literary History" (81–104) and Nina Baym's "Melodramas of Beset Manhood: How Theories of American Fiction Exclude Women Authors" (63–80), both collected in Elaine Showalter's *The New Feminist Criticism: Essays on Women, Literature and Theory* (Pantheon, 1985).

28. For a playful and astute commentary on femininity and the American novel as it relates to Oprah's Book Club (especially her choice of Franzen's *The Corrections*), see Jane Elliot's article in *Bitch* magazine (Spring 2002, pp. 70–74).

29. For a more complete discussion of the development of literary taste, see chapter four.

30. Max, p. 37.

31. Gavin McNett's comments on Oprah's Book Club appeared on *Salon*, November 12, 1999, called "Reaching to the Converted" (www.salon.com/books/feature/1999).

32. Professor Husni's quotes are, as far as I can tell, part of a larger commentary on the *Oprah* magazine (and may have been reported, as academics often are, without what he might call essential clarifying context). They are taken from an interview in the *New York Times* business section (October 2, 2000, pp. C1 and C17).

33. Mary Elizabeth Williams's counterargument to Gavin McNett's also appeared on the *Salon* site on November 12, 1999. Her piece was entitled "Silence the Snobs!" (www.salon.com/books/feature/1999). Williams had also published an earlier (May 4, 1999) defense of Oprah entitled "She's all Chat" in *Salon*'s "Brilliant Career."

Chapter Two

1. The unauthorized biographers from which I pooled this information include Janet Lowe (*Oprah Winfrey Speaks: Insights from the World's Most Influential Voice*, John Wiley, 1998), Philip Brooks (*Oprah Winfrey: A Voice for the People*, Grolier, 1999), and Bill Adler (*The Uncommon Wisdom of Oprah Winfrey: A Portrait in Her Own Words*, Citadel, 1997).

2. The Brooks quote (with its weighty tone) comes from p. 102 of his story of Oprah.

3. Oprah made reference to "the trash pack" in an article by Leonard Pitts Jr. for Knight-Ridder/Tribune News Service entitled "The Queen of Gab Leads a Campaign Against Sleaze TV" and dated July 20, 1995. This article was also quoted in Lowe, 150. It is interesting to me that she continues to make this distinction between her show and others. In a September 2002 interview with Phil Donohue in O *Magazine* (III, 9), for example, she asks Donohue a leading question about the decline of TV talk shows, and Donohue hesitates to commiserate:

> O: But don't you think some of the talk shows have gone too far? Just the other day, I was flipping through the channels and saw that people were naked on *Jerry Springer*.
>
> PD: I've been very good about trying not to sound like the old guy who says, "In my day, we'd never do that.' We were naughty too."
>
> O: I've been naughty, but some of the shows have crossed over into a whole different territory.
>
> PD: They probably have. . . .

4. Quotes from the Katie Couric interview are taken from the *Jet* cover article "Oprah Winfrey Reveals the Real Reason Why She Stayed on TV" (November 24, 1997, p. 58).

5. *Life* magazine carried a cover story "A Life in Books," in which Marilyn Johnson and Dana Fineman outlined Winfrey's reading life (September 1997).

6. Professor Gates's citation of Gronniosaw's text is from *The Signifying Monkey* (Oxford, 1988), p. 136.

7. I am also indebted to Elizabeth McHenry's *Forgotten Readers: Recovering the Lost History of African American Literary Societies* (Duke 2002) for broadening my definition of literacy to include orality in another form. While Professor

McHenry honors the fact that reading can be a transformative activity for individuals, leading to "respect, political voice, and citizenship" (83), she also describes how literacy societies allowed even those who couldn't read to benefit from the ideas in books—by listening to them. She writes:

> Reading texts aloud [as was the practice in many African American literacy societies of the nineteenth century] fostered an environment in which a truly democratic "sharing" of texts could take place, and it ensured that cohesive groups could be formed from individuals with widely divergent literacy skills. Because the process of silent reading of the text was not privileged over its oral performance, subsequent discussions could involve those who listened to the text's performances as well as those with the ability to read it for themselves. (54)

8. Toni Morrison's comments about Oprah come from the *Life* magazine article cited above.

9. Oprah lists her favorite books on her Book Club website at www.oprah.com. Of course, the website changes often, and the list of books I cite here dates from October 2000. Since then, *White Oleander* has joined the others in her top ten.

10. The third edition of the *Heath Anthology of American Literature*, Volume II, is dedicated to Elaine Hedges, longtime professor of English at Towson State University. This quote is taken from one of her introductory essays, p. 649 (Heath, 1998).

11. The article in *Good Housekeeping* (October 1996) was by Joanna Powell, and entitled "I Was Trying to Fill Something Deeper."

12. Winfrey's relationship to cultural discourses on race and the American Dream have been the subject of some fine scholarly work in articles such as Debbie Epstein and Deborah Lynn Steinburg's "American Dreamin': Discoursing Liberally on the Oprah Winfrey Show" (*Women's Studies International Forum*, v21, n1 [1998], 77–94) and Dana Cloud's "Hegemony or Concordance? Winfrey's Rags to Riches Biography" (*Critical Studies in Mass Communication* 13 [1996], 115–137). Though Oprah's life story is not the focus of my work, I address these issues further with respect to her Book Club show at the end of chapter three.

13. The published results of historian Michael Bellesiles's study of gun ownership in early America (*Arming America: The Origins of a National Gun Culture*, Knopf 2000) were a topic of controversy in the media. Professor Bellesiles

argues that, contrary to popular opinion, Americans rarely owned guns prior to the Civil War, and that the lone frontiersman cradling his rifle was mostly a mythic creation. Pioneers trapped more than hunted, and "when that brave patriot reached above the mantel, he pulled down a rusty, decaying, unusable musket (not a rifle), or found no gun at all there," he writes. Moreover, as Professor Davidson also makes clear, Americans appreciated books, and most people owned more than one. This information warms the heart of an English professor and sends me trolling for new myths—The Not-so-Lone Reader, anyone?

14. Cathy N. Davidson, who was my teacher at Michigan State University, revealingly traces book ownership and reading habits in early America in *Revolution and the Word: The Rise of the Novel in America* (Oxford, 1986). This fine study of novel reading and her careful scholarly inquiry inform my thinking and research on America's current reading habits. This quote is from p. 58.

15. Reading as "the way west" is, of course, a mythical view of our history, as much as the gun-toting frontiersman. I'm examining, here, the way the stories are told most often in mainstream cultural accounts. There are many historical exceptions to this broad brushstroke version, however. My colleague Dana D. Nelson, for example, writes in "The Word in Black and White: Ideologies of Race and Literacy in Antebellum American" (from *Reading in America: Literature and Social History*, edited by Cathy N. Davidson, Johns Hopkins, 1989, 140–156) of how "early Americans manifested a general belief in the positive link between literacy and financial gain" but makes an important point that it was not always provably so—especially for African Americans who "might be able to read Aeschylus and Homer, yet be able to procure a job no better than one as domestic help or dockworker" (152). In fact, just such a character is the focus of Rita Dove's play *Darker Face of the Earth.* Ideologies of literacy and economic progress were, in truth, often used to keep oppressive structures in place rather than to liberate Americans from them.

My thinking on the centrality of reading for democracy was also influenced by Joseph Kett's important study *The Pursuit of Knowledge Under Difficulties: From Self-Improvement to Adult Education in America, 1750–1990* (Standford University Press, 1994) which my colleague Nan Kari directed me to.

16. Joan Shelley Rubin's study "Self, Culture, and Self-Culture in Modern America: The Early History of the Book-of-the-Month Club" was first published in the *Journal of American History* (v71, n4) in March 1985. The insight about its "well-heeled audience" is from p. 789. Radway makes the point about alumni lists and the Social Register in *A Feeling for Books,* p. 295.

17. Rubin quotes Dorothy Canfield Fisher on p. 799 of her study.

18. Janice Radway writes about the Book-of-the-Month Club first in *South Atlantic Quarterly* in an article entitled "The Scandal of the Middlebrow: The Book-of-the-Month Club, Class Fracture, and Cultural Authority" (Fall 1990, 703–736). Later she published a longer study, *A Feeling for Books: The Book-of-the-Month Club, Literary Taste and Middle-Class Desire* (University of North Carolina Press, 1997). In 1989, as a PhD candidate at Michigan State University, I heard Professor Radway, also a MSU PhD and author of *Reading the Romance*, speak about BOMC. Her respectful regard for what people really read and her attention to class issues profoundly influenced my approaches to literature. In fact, such attitudes pervaded our land grant school, especially the English Department, which in 1987–1990 when I was there was still very much under the influence of the recently retired Russel B. Nye, a pathbreaker in the field of Popular Culture Studies. This quote, about the club becoming "a significant cultural trend" is from p. 704 of Radway's article in *SAQ*, and the numbers are from *A Feeling*, p. 261.

19. Any discussion of middlebrow is likely informed by Dwight MacDonald's seminal essay "Masscult and Midcult," as mine is, if only, on many points, to resist it, as I will discuss in chapter four (*Partisan Review*, Part I in Spring 1960 [203–230], and Part II in Fall 1960 [589–631]). Radway is also helpful in explaining why the middlebrow was seen as a negative or transgressive category. She writes, "The middlebrow was formed, rather, as a category, by processes of literary and cultural mixing whereby forms and values associated with one form of cultural production were wed to forms and values usually connected with another. Thus . . . the scandal of the middlebrow was a function of its failure to maintain the fences cordoning off culture from commerce, the sacred from the profane, and the low from the high" (152). I also discuss this idea further in chapter four.

I also found Nicola Humble's recent work *The Feminine Middlebrow Novel 1920s to 1950s: Class Domesticity and Bohemianism* (Oxford, 2001) informative about the gendered nature of the middlebrow. Humble notes that the term "middlebrow" was used "as a form of disapprobation, suggesting a smug 'easy' read, lacking significant intellectual challenges." She adds, "For many who applied the term, one suspects that the central tenet that allowed a novel to be dismissed as middlebrow was the issue of whom it was read by: once a novel became widely popular, it became suspect, and bestseller status, or adoption as a Book-of-the-Month choice by a major book club was sufficient to demote it beneath serious attention. A novel was therefore middlebrow not because of any intrinsic content, but because it was widely read by the middle-class public—and particularly the lower middle classes" (13). She also notes that "virtually all women's writing of the period in question (with the standard exception of Virginia Woolf) was treated as middlebrow" (15).

I am indebted, as well, to Jamie Harker, of the University of Mississippi, for conversations and essays that deepened my understanding of what made popular novels middlebrow in this time period.

And now, years later, I'm indebted to the early Rhoda, who I ended up liking much better than Mary.

20. The *OED* definition of "middlebrow" from *Punch* is quoted in Radway, *A Feeling*, p. 219. Humble's definition of middlebrow is also good: "the middlebrow novel is one that straddles the divide between the trashy romance or thriller on one hand, and the philosophically or formally challenging novel on the other: offering narrative excitement without guilt, and intellectual stimulation without undue effort" (11).

21. Radway, "The Scandal," p. 726.

22. Poetry, of course, has an alternative personality from the highbrow modernist mode of T. S. Eliot. In United States culture, there has long been a tradition of doggerel, or rhyming verse, on greeting cards and in popular magazines, and sentimental free verse circulates unfettered on the Internet and in popular publications. Often a book of poetry that critics would never deign to address becomes quite popular—witness the success of Oprah's own Mattie Stepanek. However, I find, generally, that my students are intimidated by poetry, that they find it difficult and mysterious, and are afraid they "don't get it." That is the legacy of its highbrow identity.

23. Davidson, p. 73.

24. This quote comes at the end of a chapter, "Small Temptations," at the center of the novel, both literally and thematically (*Rose in Bloom*, Little Brown, 1876, p. 193).

25. Davidson, p. 66.

26. Nina Baym used the quote from *Harper's Magazine*, June 1853, in her excellent study *Novels, Readers, and Reviewers: Responses to Fiction in Antebellum America* (Cornell, 1984, p. 28). The phrase "union of popularity and artistry" is also from Baym, p. 44.

27. Davidson, p. 79.

28. I begin quoting Baym directly after Davidson in this paragraph with the concept of the "spirit of the age" (pp. 14, 44).

29. Quotes from the Book Club Programs are culled both from the transcripts (again, from Burrelle's Transcripts, Livingston, NJ) and from my homemade tapes of the shows. Thus, my quotes may sometimes differ slightly from the transcript version. This *Song of Solomon* discussion is mainly true to the transcript version. The Book Club is the second half of a show titled "How'd They Do That?" November 18, 1996.

30. Winfrey introduced *Stones from the River* at the end of the *She's Come Undone* Book Club meeting. The transcript is titled "3rd Rock From the Sun," February 28, 1997.

31. The quote from the introduction to *Here on Earth* comes at the end of the discussion of *Paradise*, March 6, 1998.

32. The quote from the introduction to the Kaye Gibbons's books comes at the end of the transcript titled "Oprah's Book Club Goes to Louisiana," October 27, 1997.

33. The idea of *Paradise* as gourmet meal is cited in the transcript "Bill Cosby," January 16, 1998.

34. "I liked it a lot!" is from the first Book Club Meeting, the second half of the show titled "Pregnant Women Who Use Drugs and Alcohol," September 17, 1996.

35. Elizabeth Long has been, for some time, the most significant researcher and thinker on the phenomenon of women's book clubs in the United States. At the time I completed this manuscript, her book, *Book Clubs: Women and the Uses of Reading in Everyday Life*, had just been published by the University of Chicago Press. Professor Long generously shared parts of her unpublished manuscript with me, and my work is also informed by Long's previously published works, including "Women, Reading, and Cultural Authority: Some Implications of the Audience Perspective in Cultural Studies" in *American Quarterly* (v38, n4 [Fall 1986], 591–612), "The Book as Mass Commodity: The Audience Perspective" in *Book Research Quarterly* (Spring 1987, 9–30), "Reading Groups and The Postmodern Crisis of Cultural Authority" in *Cultural Studies* (v1, n3 [October 1987], 306–327), "Textual Interpretation as Collective Action" in *Discourse* (v14, n3 [Summer 1992], 104–130), and *The American Dream and the Popular Novel* (Routledge, 1985).

Long explains in "Textual Interpretation" the academic's preference for reflective reading: "Academics tend to repress consideration of variety in reading practices due to our assumptions that everyone reads (or ought to) as we do professionally, privileging the cognitive, ideational, and analytic mode." Recognizing variety, especially in collective reading practices such as those in book groups, "inevitably brings into view both the commercial underside of literature and the scholar's position of authority in the world or reading" (116). I will return to this connection to the commercial in chapter four.

36. The idea of women operating comfortably in empathic modes figures prominently in various feminist studies, most significantly, in my reading, from Carol Gilligan's *In a Different Voice: Psychological Theory and Women's Development* (Harvard, 1982), Nancy Chodorow's *The Reproduction of Mothering: Psychoanalysis and the Sociology of Gender* (University of California, 1978), and Sarah Ruddick's *Maternal Thinking: Toward a Politics of Peace* (Ballantine, 1989). I am also influenced, in this exploration of reading modes, by reader-response criticism, especially the feminist work of Elizabeth A. Flynn and Patricinio P. Schweickart, which I first encountered in graduate school and have been thinking about ever since. Schweickart, particularly, begins valuing a conversation model of reading early on, at the end of her important essay "Reading Ourselves: Toward a Feminist Theory of Reading" (in *Gender and Reading* [John Hopkins 1986]).

37. The quotes from the *Song of Solomon* meeting are taken directly from the transcript (see note 29, ch. 2).

38. *Paradise* quotes are from the transcript "Book Club—Toni Morrison," March 6, 1998.

39. Radway discusses a similar diversity of approaches to reading at the Book-of-the-Month Club in *A Feeling for Books*. She writes, "The modality of reading privileged at the Book-of-the-Month Club emphasized both sense and sensibility, both affect and cognition. It mobilized the body and the brain, the heart and the soul. It as a mode of reading that stressed immersion and connection, communication and response" (117).

40. David Richter discusses "reading for fun" and "reading for class" in *Falling into Theory* (Bedford 1999). See note 28, ch. 3.

Chapter Three _____

1. The term "oprahfication," according to commentator Mark Steyn, is "nothing less than the wholesale makeover of the nation, and then the world." Quoting the *Wall Street Journal*, he adds that it began as "public confession as a form of therapy," and notes that "not many TV performers are privileged to be-

come nouns and adjectives." Steyn's commments appear in "Comic Oprah" in *National Review*, March 23, 1998, p. 30.

2. Harold Bloom, from *How to Read and Why* (Scribner, 2000) p. 22.

3. Judith Shulevitz's article "You Read Your Book and I'll Read Mine" appeared in the *New York Times Book Review* on May 19, 2002.

4. All of the book groups meeting "as you read this sentence" can't be estimated accurately, as Elizabeth Long discovered when her estimate of groups meeting in Houston, Texas, went from twelve to 121 to "impossible to count reliably" (xiv). She points out that "there has been an almost explosive growth in the number of women participating in informal reading groups since the 1980s" (19), a fact affirmed by media attention to the book group phenomenon and by the attention publishing houses have begun paying to these groups. Not only do they include lists of questions for book groups at the end of many contemporary novels, but they also send representatives out to bookstores to meet with book groups and offer reading suggestions. One local independent bookstore here in St. Paul advertises these visits in their newsletter, along with readings by visiting writers.

5. Elizabeth Long also makes the case for social reading effectively in "Textual Interpretation as Collective Action" (*Discourse* 14.3), in which she contrasts a solitary reader with a group of readers. She writes, "Even beyond formal socialization into reading, the habit of reading is profoundly social. As mid-century American empirical studies of adult reading show, social isolation depresses readership, and social involvement encourages it. Most readers need the support of talk with other readers, the participation in a social milieu in which books are 'in the air'" (109). The quote in my text is also from this article, p. 112; the concluding quote is taken from the unpublished synopsis of "Women Reading Together: Book Groups, Subjectivity, and Social Change," provided by the author.

6. *The Book Group Book: A Thoughtful Guide to Forming and Enjoying a Stimulating Book Discussion Group*, edited by Ellen Slezak (3rd edition, Chicago Review Press, 2000). Neidorf's comments come from pp. 27 and 30 of that collection. Slezak also dedicates the book to her mom "who is rarely without a book in hand."

7. Kathryn Lampher on her "Midmorning" program "The Power of Women in Bookstores" on MPR January 9, 2002 (www.mpr.org). She can now be heard with Al Franken on "The O'Franken Factor" on Air America Radio.

8. I am referring here to the work of feminist historians such as Caroll Smith-Rosenberg, Nancy F. Cott, Sara Evans, Linda Kerber, Alice Kessler-Harris, and Laurel Thatcher Ulrich.

9. T. S. Eliot from "The Love Song of J. Alfred Prufrock." Writer Frank Norris also disdainfully describes a group of club women in an 1896 essay:

> The consider themselves literary. . . . after graduation they "read papers" to "literary circles" composed of post-graduate "co-eds," the professors' wives and daughters and a very few pale young men in spectacles and black cutaway coats. After the reading of the "paper" follows the "discussion," aided and abetted by cake and lemonade. This is literature! Isn't it admirable! (qtd in Gere, p. 214)

10. Though this summary is influenced by the work of feminist historians listed earlier, as well as by the work of my colleague Jane Carroll, professor of history at College of St. Catherine, much of it is culled from Gere's summary in *Intimate Practices: Literacy and Cultural Work in U.S. Women's Clubs, 1880–1920* (Urbana: U of Illinois P: 1997)

11. Margaret Atwood from *The Book Group Book*, p. xi.

12. Gere, p. 35.

13. Gere, p. 17.

14. Long, "Textual Interpretation," p. 112.

15. Frances Devlin-Glass from "More than a Reader and Less than a Critic: Literary Authority and Women's Book-Discussion Groups" (*Women's Studies International Forum* v 24, n5 [2001], pp. 571–585), p. 583.

16. Edie Jaye Cohen, *Book Group Book*, p. 65; Rose, p. 66; Wuebbeler, p. 67.

17. Hustedde, *Book Group Book*, p. 143.

18. Ewing, *Book Group Book*, p. 11. Janet Tripp also compares her group with such stereotypes later in the collection. She writes, "We don't wear white gloves, flowered hats, and nylon stockings with seams snaking up the backs of our calves" (162).

19. Thelen and Vick, *Book Group Book*, p. 55.

20. Tripp, *Book Group Book*, p. 159. This word "communion" appears in several reflections I have read from readers who participate in book clubs—

reflecting, I think, something deeper than connection or community. Another example is in an article by Patrick McCormick for *U.S. Catholic* (February 1997), in which he uses Oprah's Book Club as a springboard to reflect on his own book clubs:

> . . . the reading group has made reading literature a social event for me, or at least allowed the solitude of reading a good book to blossom into a conversation—even a sort of communion—with other persons. . . . Indeed, as I sit down to read each new book, a growing part of the pleasure of reading comes from anticipating how John or Alexis might respond to a particular passage, or remembering a comment Scott or Debbie made about a similar text. Even in the act of reading I am not alone. (40)

21. My Utah and Minnesota book groups continue to inspire my confidence in the importance of social reading.

22. The Morrison quote is from *Paradise* transcript "Book Club—Toni Morrison," March 6, 1998.

23. Website at www.oprah.com in March 2002

24. Winfrey's comments are from transcript entitled "Oprah's Book Club: *Drowning Ruth*," November 16, 2000. Quotes also from my tape.

25. Transcript and tape of the Book Club meeting on *Black and Blue*, May 22, 1998.

26. Transcript entitled "Oprah's Book Club: *Open House* Discussion," September 27, 2000. This quote, however comes from my tape.

27. Jane Tompkins, *Sensational Designs: The Cultural Work of American Fiction 1790–1860* (Oxford, 1985), p. 200.

28. For a more complete (and highly readable) summary of this conflict in literary studies, see David Richter's *Falling into Theory* (2nd edition, Bedford/St. Martin's, 2000), a book I use as an introductory text for my English majors to "teach them the conflicts," as Gerald Graff famously stated. It could be argued that this conflict is at the base of the "Culture War" in the humanities over the past decade. Though the change came earlier when schools began accommodating their diverse students with texts from many cultures, the response began with Allan Bloom's *The Closing of the American Mind*, and his conservative argument that students are losing out because teachers have quit teaching the central texts of Western culture. Arguments for and against literary theory, postmodernism, and multiculturalism have been common over the past twenty years in colleges

and universities and at academic conferences in the humanities. Of the many treatments of the controversies, I have found Michael Bérubé and Cary Nelson's *Higher Education Under Fire: Politics, Economics, and the Crisis of the Humanities* (Routledge, 1995) most helpful. I also consulted John Guillory's *Cultural Capital: The Problem of Literary Canon Formation* (University of Chicago, 1993, and the excerpt from it that I teach in Richter's *The Critical Tradition: Classic Texts and Contemporary Trends*, 2nd ed., Bedford, 1998) and Richard Ohmann's *Selling Culture: Magazines, Markets and Class at the Turn of the Century* (Verso, 1996, and the essay that first appeared in *Critical Inquiry*). I also discuss this conflict in chapter four.

29. Letters from the *Open House* dinner guests were still available on the website at the time of this writing.

30. Transcript entitled "Oprah's Book Club: Open House Discussion," September 27, 2000. Quotes from my tape.

31. D. T. Max wrote "The Oprah Effect" for the *New York Times Magazine*, December 26, 1999, p. 41.

32. It can't be disputed that many Oprah fans like the Book Club for the same reason they would like anything that Oprah sponsors. As Patricia Sellers noted in *Fortune* Magazine (v145, n7 [April 1, 2002], 50+), "Oprah's life is the essence of her brand."

33. In an interview with a representative of Harpo in June 2002, the spokesperson reported that they received thousands of letters for each book. "It varies from book to book but is in the thousands for every book," she told me. She noted that the variations were affected by book choice, but also by how long readers had to respond between book announcements.

34. *The Bluest Eye* quotes are taken mainly from my tape of the program, May 26, 2000. Introductions to the guests on this show were still available online as of March 2003.

35. As Janice Peck carefully outlines in her article, "Talk About Racism: Framing a Popular Discourse of Race on Oprah Winfrey" (*Cultural Critique* [Spring 1994] pp. 89–126), the Book Club program on *The Bluest Eye* isn't the first time Oprah addressed the topic of racism on her program. Peck studies "Racism in 1992," a yearlong, thirteen-episode treatment of racism on Oprah's show. In this forum, as Peck points out, Oprah's approach focuses on changing perceptions, rather than changing institutions, just as it does in this Book Club episode.

36. Maya Angelou's Book Club meeting transcript is called "Book Club Finale," June 18, 1997, and September 1, 1997.

37. The students in my Summer 2002 section of "The Novel: Oprah's Book Club," had a heyday with the new book clubs popping up in the wake of Oprah's sign-off. The network morning shows were especially active participants with Katie Couric and Matt Lauer, Regis Philbin and Kelly Ripa, and Charles Gibson and Diane Sawyer all jumping on the Book Club bandwagon. None of these book clubs have had the audience, the selling power, or the staying power of Oprah's Book Club. None of them take books or readers as seriously as Oprah did, as demonstrated by the short time they spend on their selections and the even shorter time they allow for reader commentary. Ripa, in fact, capitalized on the idea that her books would be entertaining rather than edifying. As *PW Daily* (Tuesday, May 21, 2002) noted, "Setting the agenda, a quick video lead-in for the [first book club] segment shows Ripa, eyes wide open in astonishment, peeking over the edge of a hardcover book as the words fun, quick, sexy and juicy appeared."

38. Like many book club members, what I missed most on Oprah's Book Club was the level of disagreement that often comes in discussions of contemporary novels. Readers who disliked the novel seldom appeared on the program (see discussion of *White Oleander* in chapter four); this is, I surmise, a function of the TV talk show format, which requires a level of focus and coherence that the book groups I know could never tolerate. For further discussion of this point, see the Conclusion.

39. Oprah's embodiment of the American Dream has been a controversial point in academic treatments of her work. Dana L. Cloud, in "Hegemony or Concordance? The Rhetoric of Tokenism in 'Oprah' Winfrey's Rags-to-Riches Biography" (*Critical Studies in Mass Communication* 13 [1996], pp. 115–137), for example, makes a strong case that Oprah's story is an example of capitalist society's tokenism. Making Oprah a representative of an entire race or class, American society then holds that race or class accountable for their own failures, thereby using the language of liberal individualism to deny any responsibility for structural and institutional inequities. Oprah's story, she argues, "resonates with and reinforces the ideology of the American Dream, implying the accessibility of this dream" to American women, African Americans, and the lower class.

Debbie Epstein and Deborah Lynn Steinberg conduct a similar discussion of Oprah's position as representative of the American Dream in their article "American Dreamin': Discoursing Liberally on the Oprah Winfrey Show" (*Women's Studies International Forum* 21:1 [1998], pp. 77–95). They argue that the iconographic status of the Oprah Winfrey show rests on the "seductiveness" of the American Dream, concluding that: "At one level, the Oprah Winfrey Show seems, more often than not, to sustain the happy, sappy myth of the American Dream and to speak from, to, and bespeak the soft center of bourgeois liberalism with its, at best misleading and at worst, disingenuous claims to democracy, equality, and opportunity. At the same time, in the frame of the American Dream, it is also the dispossessed who are the subjects of the narrative and have their own voices within it" (92). I appreciate this caveat more than the conclusion of either article, which I find somewhat jaded. A belief in the voices of those "dispossessed" serves as the foundation of my argument in the concluding chapter of this study—that those subjects, the talking readers, used Oprah's forum powerfully and successfully to challenge given cultural wisdom, and to refigure the way Americans read and value novels. This is not to say I would undermine, generally, the argument that this emphasis on individual rather than larger social phenomenon is not helpful, as we have seen, nor do I deny, generally, the power of capitalism to maintain inequities and an oppressive social status quo. I just find holes in the hegemony.

I also found insightful commentary on Oprah's position in consumer culture in an unpublished manuscript "Commodification, Difference, and Discipline: Oprah's Book Club and African American-Literature" by Roderick A. Ferguson, a sociologist at UCSD. Thanks to Teresa Swartz, formerly of the St. Kate's Women's Studies program, for that connection.

Chapter Four _____

1. Jonathan Franzen, "Perchance to Dream: In the Age of Images, a Reason to Write Novels" (*Harper's Magazine*, v292, n1751 [April 1996], pp. 35–.

2. Franzen from an interview with Powell's Bookstore in Portland, Oregon, pulled from their website in October 2001. Also qtd. in a *New York Times* article (October 24, 2001, p. C4), "Winfrey Rescinds Offer to Author for Guest Appearance" by David Kirkpatrick.

3. Oprah's comments appeared in a terse statement linked to the Book Club page on her website in October 2001.

4. I followed the story in the *New York Times* (see reference below), but articles also appeared in *The Chronicle of Higher Education* (November 30, 2001), *People*—twice (November 12, 2001 and December 31, 2001), *The New York Observer* (November 1, 2001), *Newsweek* (November 5, 2001), *The Library Journal* (November 15, 2001), *The New Yorker* (December 16, 2001), regularly

in *Publishers Weekly* through October and November 2001, and in various other places.

5. Some examples of early reviews of *The Corrections* include: *Publishers Weekly* (v248, n29 [July 16, 2001] p. 164): "This is, simply, a masterpiece"; *Booklist* (v97 n21 [July 2001] p. 1947): "Heir in scope and spirit to the great nineteenth-century novelists . . ."; *Library Journal* (v126, n13 [August 2001], p. 160): "In this novel of breathtaking virtuosity . . ."; *Book* (September 2001): *The Corrections* "is not only the author's funniest and most focused work, it also hits harder and deeper"; *Fortune* (v144, n4 [September 3, 2001] p. 256): "Harrowing and hysterical, *The Corrections* is the novel of the year"; *The Economist* (September 8, 2001), which panned it, but with this language: "A Great American novel has been expected from Jonathan Franzen since the mid-westerner first appeared on the New York literary scene . . . and this novel proves to be truly great in length alone"; even *O Magazine*, which called it a "dazzling new novel" before Oprah chose it.

6. Publishing numbers came from Laurie Brown, vice-president for marketing at Farrar, Straus, qtd. in a *New York Times* article (October 21, 2001, p. 6) "On the Dust Jacket, to O or Not to O" by Monica Corcoran.

7. Franzen, from an NPR interview, pulled from the website (NPR.org) in October 2001, also qtd. in *New York Times* article (October 21, 2001, p. 6) "On the Dust Jacket, to O or Not to O" by Monica Corcoran.

8. Corcoran article (see previous note).

9. Franzen, qtd. in a *New York Times* article (October 24, 2001, p. C4), "Winfrey Rescinds Offer to Author for Guest Appearance" by David Kirkpatrick.

10. Franzen, qtd. in a *New York Times* article (October 29, 2001, p. E1), "'Oprah' Gaffe by Franzen Draws Ire and Sales" by David Kirkpatrick.

11. One of the best discussions I have read of how Oprah bridged the divide behind high and low culture as high culture critics bridled was Kathy Rooney's article in the *Nation* (May 20, 2002, pp. 56+) just as the Book Club ended.

12. Rick Moody, qtd. in a *New York Times* article (October 29, 2001, p. E1), "Oprah Gaffe by Franzen Draws Ire and Sales" by David Kirkpatrick.

13. The spokesperson for Harpo, Inc. in the June 2001 interview explained that the publishers were the ones who requested permission to put the

Oprah O on their book covers, and "we granted permission." She added, "We don't require anyone to print that information [the Oprah O] on the book." Later, they asked for permission to reprint books with the logo embedded in the cover art. "The publishers were anxious to get that information on the book," she said.

She also told me that "the Book Club shows on average have slightly lower ratings than the other shows." Ratings winners, she explained were "celebrity shows" or "shows with Dr. Phil." When the Book Club drew a respectable audience, Oprah "was frankly so delighted and pleased when people *were* watching" because "she didn't expect it." From the beginning, she said (and Oprah has confirmed in other interviews) that Oprah wasn't sure the Book Club would work, "but she was committed to trying it anyway."

14. The publishers' reluctance to say anything against Oprah was reflected in a *New York Observer* article by Gabriel Snyder (November 1, 2001). "One New York editor" is quoted as saying, "When I ever even come close to voicing any sympathy [for Mr. Franzen], I am actually shouted down—even people I am intimate with, who would tell me the truth. . . . There seems to be a genuine siding in the literary community with Oprah."

15. Bloom, qtd. in a *New York Times* article (October 29, 2001, p. E1), "'Oprah' Gaffe by Franzen Draws Ire and Sales" by David Kirkpatrick.

16. Again, like the tradition of the American novel, the idea of cultural capital is central to the postmodern theory that I specialize in and teach, so the comments I make here are influenced by fifteen years worth of sources, many of which I probably can't name or remember, but those I continue to find fascinating and influential are the works of Bourdieu (especially *Distinction*), Radway (*A Feeling*), Raymond Williams (*Marxism and Literature*), Jennifer Scanlon (*The Gender and Consumer Culture Reader*), and John Guillory (*Cultural Capital: The Problem of Literary Canon Formation*). For this chapter, I also consulted Eric Schlosser's *Fast Food Nation*. Other sources are cited below.

17. The idea of associating middlebrow novels with kitsch can be traced in part to Dwight MacDonald's dismissive and influential assessment of the middlebrow in the two-part "Masscult and Midcult" (*Partisan Review*, Part I in Spring 1960 [203–230], and Part II in Fall 1960 [589–631]) (See note 19, ch. 2). When high and low cultures are distinct, he argues, as art and kitsch, things work. But let in the wretched middlebrow, and things fall apart. "The problem is especially acute in this country because class lines are especially weak here. If there were a clearly defined cultural elite here, then the masses

could have their *kitsch* and the classes could have their high culture with everybody happy. But a significant part of our population is chronically confronted with a choice between looking at TV or old masters, between reading Tolstoy or a detective story; i.e., the pattern of their cultural lives is open to the point of being porous" (II, 589). The Midcult, containing elements of both kitsch and class, has filled up the space in between, to the detriment of everyone, and, he argues, should be eliminated. "It is not just unsuccessful art. It is non-art. It is even anti-art. (I, 204). He concludes, "So let the masses have their Masscult, let the few who care about good writing, painting, music, architecture, philosophy, etc., have their High Culture, and don't fuzz up the distinction with Midcult" (II, 628).

18. Max, p. 40.

19. Lapham qtd. in a *New York Times* article (October 29, 2001, p. E1), "'Oprah' Gaffe by Franze Draws Ire and Sales" by David Kirkpatrick.

20. Most early Book Clubs included (somewhat disruptive) comments about the food, the chef, and the restaurant or other venue where the meeting was held. The *Deep End of the Ocean* Book Club ("Newborn Quintuplets Come Home," October 18, 1996) was held at Oprah's house over wild mushroom ravioli and "crème brulée with fresh raspberries and caramel shortbread cookies." The *Stones from the River* meeting ("Selena's Family," April 8, 1997), held in a public library in Riverside, Illinois, featured the seared yellow-tailed tuna.

21. Oprah from transcript entitled "Bill Cosby," January 16, 1998.

22. Michael Korda, *Making the List: A Cultural History of the American Bestseller 1900–1999* (New York: Barnes and Noble, 2001), p. x.

23. Korda, p. xxi.

24. Radway "The Scandal," p. 711.

25. Radway, *A Feeling for Books*, pp. 210, 227.

26. Bloom, *How to Read and Why*, p. 238. I don't know about you, but I can find many, many literary characters who are better models of a prototypical American than the self-absorbed and obsessive Ahab. Even Gatsby would be better. But I'll take Zora Neale Hurston's Janie or Willa Cather's Antonia. There's the topic. Talk amongst yourselves.

27. Bloom, pp. 20, 22.

28. Bloom, pp. 159, 160.

29. From *How to Read a Book: A Classic Guide to Intelligent Reading* by Mortimer Adler and Charles Van Doren (Simon and Schuster, 1972), p. 8. I selected this book, along with Bloom's, because they are the guides for general readers I found most often in bookstores. Though this guide clearly does not reflect contemporary approaches to literature, it continues to be influential and sells well. I also appreciate Mortimer Adler's often-stated commitment to the general reader, a commitment that led him to such a project as *How to Read a Book*. Though his methods eventually undermine his aims, I honor what I understand to be the original spirit of the work.

30. Adler and Van Doren, p. 350.

31. Bourdieu, 1 and throughout (especially chapter 1, Conclusion, and Postscript).

32. Another recent phenomenon a group of my students discovered in their research project is the more frequent appearance of Reading Group Guides at the end of contemporary novels, especially, they found, novels by women. William McGinley and Kattana Conley discuss these guides in "Literary Retailing and the (Re)Making of Popular Reading" in the *Journal of Popular Culture* (Fall 2001) as another way of training inexperienced readers to read in traditional academic modes, despite their appearance of valuing popular modes. On the other hand, my students valued the difference in tone between these guides at the end of books versus "critical introductions" at the beginning that guide your reading from the start, not just question you later about if you saw "the right things."

33. Adler and Van Doren, p. 204.

34. Adler and Van Doren, p. 213.

35. Bloom, p. 196.

36. Adler and Van Doren, p. 214.

37. Douglas B. Holt, "Does Cultural Capital Structure American Consumption?" in *The Consumer Society Reader*, Juliet B. Schor and Douglas B. Holt, eds. (New Press, 2000, pp. 212–252), p. 218.

38. Holt, p. 219.

39. Holt, p. 239.

40. These student comments are taken from journal entries and final exams, which they agreed to allow me to use if I did not cite their names. Students in all five sections of "The Novel: Oprah's Book Club" that I have taught

since 1998 were aware that they were involved in and contributing to my research. Indeed, all of them completed final research projects that inform aspects of my work, including the list of Oprah's Book topics from chapter one and the update on new TV book groups in chapter three, among other projects. Perhaps the most interesting have been projects linking public reading to public spaces, like the coffeeshops my students are required to meet in regularly for small group work. For further information about the course, see the sample syllabi on my web page at www.stkate.edu and a list of student names in the Acknowledgments. Again, I want to acknowledge my indebtedness to these students for their challenging questions and fascinating work. This book would not have happened without them.

41. Wendy Steiner in "Look Who's Modern Now" in the *New York Times Book Review* (October 10, 1999).

42. Radway recalls in *Feeling for Books* that, before she became a professionally trained critic, "the act of reading was propelled more by a driving desire to know, to connect, to communicate, and to share than by the desires to evaluate, to explicate, to explain, to discriminate, and judge" (7).

43. I have never gotten completely satisfactory answers about Oprah's selection process, though the D. T. Max article from the *New York Times Magazine* cited in chapter one comes closest. The spokesperson I interviewed at Harpo, Inc. explained the selection process as follows: "The process is simple. She reads a book. She loves it. She picks it." She added that a friend or neighbor will sometimes "put a book in Oprah's hand," and that Oprah regularly reads the *New York Times Book Review* looking for good suggestions. The spokesperson also acknowledged, "she does have a staff who read books for the purpose of passing on suggestions to her, but Oprah chooses every book." Oprah's only requirement, she insisted, is that "her recommendations need to be heartfelt."

44. Malcolm Gladwell, "The Coolhunt" in *The Consumer Society Reader*, Juliet B. Schor and Douglas B. Holt, eds. (New Press, 2000, pp. 360–374), p. 365.

45. Faith Popcorn, *EVEolution: The Eight Truths of Marketing to Women* (Hyperion, 2000), pp. 5, 17, and throughout. Popcorn's book, which has its own vocabulary list to translate the Popcorny language, includes this astute quote about Oprah: "Oprah brought women together in a network around higher values, sharing common ground. . . . Oprah's power lie in her fundamental understanding of the need that women have to be emotionally bonded to each other." Is it any accident that her own book is entitled, *Make the Connection*"? (24).

46. Phil Donohue was known for moving away from shows dominated by professional "experts" into talk shows where the audience starred. In an interview with Oprah (*O Magazine*, v3, n9 [September 2002]), Oprah says, "You started all of this!" and he replies, "If that's what you think, I'm proud. What I'm most proud of is that we involved the audience more than anybody else in the game. People who owned the airwaves got to actually use them in this wild thing called democracy. Hooray for us" (279).

I should also note here that my understanding of the talk show format is informed by several impressive academic studies of how women talk on *Oprah!*, most of which emphasize the connectedness and empathy I have discussed here. Among these are articles by Corinne Squire ("Oprah Winfrey and the Construction of Intimacy in the Talk Show Setting" in *Journal of Popular Culture*, pp. 115–121) and Laurie Haag ("Empowering Women? The Oprah Winfrey Show" in *Feminist Television Criticism* [Oxford, 1997] pp. 98–117), but I especially appreciated Gloria-Jean Masciarotte's work, specifically, in this context, "C'mon Girl: Oprah Winfrey and the Discourse of Feminine Talk" (*Genders* 11 [Fall 1991], pp. 81–110).

An interesting new academic treatise by Irene Kacandes called *Talk Fiction: Literature and the Talk Explosion* (University of Nebraska, 2000) explores talking or "secondary orality" as a quality of fiction. She discusses "works of twentieth century narrative literature that promote a sense of relationship and exchange in readers that we normally associate with face-to-face interaction" (1). I found her observations on talk shows and "the general rise of participatory talk practices and the multiplication of 'talk spaces' in the West" especially productive (19). Though the bulk of her study concerns how certain texts promote "talk reading," the connections she makes throughout with "participatory talk shows" and the "sense of readers as active participants and of stories as social tasks" affirms the changing modes of reading that I, too, found key to twentieth-century reading practices (34). However, citing Robin Lakoff's work, she seems, at times, to set up a model that would oppose orality with literacy, a model I don't accept, and that her textual examples defy (21).

47. Of course, I can't hide that my hope is that readers, with practice in reflective reading skills, will eventually seek out Woolf or Morrison themselves. But I can't deny that I found great pleasure in reading *What Looks Like Crazy on an Ordinary Day*, and other such books I never would have encountered without paying attention to empathic or inspirational standards of literary merit.

48. Franzen, pp. 6, 4.

49. Franzen, p. 5.

50. I appreciated Martha C. Nussbaum's argument in *Cultivating Humanity: A Classical Defense of Reform in Liberal Education* (Harvard University Press, 1997) that revisited nineteenth-century novels of George Eliot and Charles Dickens to argue that a "commitment to the making of a social world, and of a deliberate community to think critically about, is what makes the adventure of reading so fascinating, and so urgent" (104). Her major point in "Chapter Three: The Narrative Imagination" is that arguments against canon revision that base their claims in "an extreme kind of aesthetic formalism" that she links to "a relatively narrow and recent history. . . namely the Kantian and post-Kantian formalist tradition" (102) attempt to deny that "the Western aesthetic tradition has had throughout its history an intense concern with character and community" (89). She sees this as a gross misrepresentation of the Western tradition as it comes to us from the Greeks onward of "the political promise of literature" for engaged citizens. She writes:

> It is the political promise of literature that it can transport us, while remaining ourselves, into the life of another, revealing similarities but also profound differences between the life and thought of that other and myself . . . Any stance toward criticism that denies that possibility seems to deny the very possibility of literary experience as a human social good (111).

I admire the way she uses arguments from both sides of the Culture Wars to stake out a position that values various aspects of literary experience, including the social. In doing this, she cites the arguments of Wayne Booth in *The Company We Keep*, and of reader-response critics generally. It will be apparent to many readers that my position, which similarly affirms the social aspects of novels, is informed by reader-response criticism, which I have read and valued for years, as well as by Booth's *The Rhetoric of Fiction*.

Conclusion _____

1. I saw the phrase "The American Century" used repeatedly in the final years of the twentieth century and in the endless journalistic and academic roundups published in 2000 and 2001, and Wolfe uses it frequently in his discussion.

2. *Moral Freedom: The Search for Virtue in a World of Choice* (Norton, 2001), Alan Wolfe, pp. 199–200 and throughout.

3. David Brooks in *Bobos in Paradise: The New Upper Class and How They Got There* (Simon and Schuster, 2000), p. 233.

4. Brooks, p. 234.

5. Brooks, p. 243.

6. Though I tend to trust my students, who grew up in a postmodern world, for conceptual clarity about postmodernism, there is also a theoretical foundation for this discussion, most significantly from Jean-Francois Lyotard's *The Postmodern Condition: A Report on Knowledge* (Minneapolis: U of Minnesota P, 1989). Other texts that have shaped my understanding of postmodernism include Linda Hutcheon's *A Poetics of Postmodernism: History, Theory, Ficton* (Routledge, 1988), and various essays from the text I use to teach my postmodernist theory course: David Richter's *The Critical Tradition: Classic Texts and Contemporary Trends* (2nd ed., Bedford, 1998).

7. Paul Lauter said this about literary standards in *Reconstructing American Literature: Courses, Syllabi, Issues*, which he edited (Feminist P, 1983), p. xvii.

8. Brooks, p. 242.

9. Wolfe, p. 226.

10. Elizabeth Long points out that the white middle-class book club members she studies "generally accept without question the categories of classification and evaluation generated by cultural arbiters such as reviewers or professors. Their acceptance of this evaluative framework as the criterion for demarcating what is worth discussing from trash is the clearest evidence of their dependence on cultural authority" (*Book Clubs*, 118). However, Long also notes that when these women discuss books, they often challenge these standards. One book club member commented, "Maybe we should be the ones to decide if a book's a classic. If it generates good discussion, it's a classic" (151).

11. Barbara Herrnstein Smith in *Contingencies of Value: Alternative Perspectives for Critical Theory* (Harvard UP, 1988).

12. Bourdieu, p. 34.

13. I first ran into the term "discussability" as I interviewed book group members informally. It also appears in Long's and Devlin-Glass's work (in interviews with book group members).

14. The spokesperson from Harpo told me (in our July 11, 2002 interview) that Oprah loves this story of the woman who read along with the Book Club—but with completely different books. She said, as far as Oprah is concerned, "the more people reading the better. It doesn't have to be the books she chooses."

15. Quotations from the *White Oleander* discussion, June 15, 1999, come from my transcription of the show. Student comments are from my Summer 1999 and Summer 2002 sections of Oprah Books, the two sections that read *White Oleander*. The passage quoted from the book is from 157.

16. Again, the focused discussion that characterizes the Book Group dinner meetings may simply be a function of the talk show format and its careful construction around one or two main ideas. I suspect that Oprah could have gathered readers who challenged the novel's aesthetic merit, but she chose instead (and again) to people the dinner with readers who would be most interested in the novel's social issues—foster mothers and former foster children.

17. "Ozymandias" by Percy Bysshe Shelley, 1818.

Works Cited

Adler, Bill, ed. *The Uncommon Wisdom of Oprah Winfrey: A Portrait in her Own Words* (unauthorized). Secaucus, NJ: Citadel, 1997.

Adler, Mortimer J., and Charles Van Doren. *How to Read a Book: A Classic Guide to Intelligent Reading.* New York: Simon and Schuster, 1940. Updated edition, 1972.

Alcott, Louisa May. *Rose in Bloom.* New York: Burt, 1876.

Atwood, Margaret. "Foreward" to *The Book Group Book: A Thoughtful Guide to Forming and Enjoying a Stimulating Book Discussion Group*, 3rd ed. Ellen Slezak, ed. Chicago: Chicago Review P, 2000.

Baym, Nina. "Melodramas of Beset Manhood: How Theories of American Fiction Exclude Women Authors" in *The New Feminist Criticism: Women, Literature, Theory.* Elaine Showalter, ed. New York: Pantheon, 1985. 63–80.

———. *Novels, Readers, and Reviewers: Reponses to Fiction in Antebellum America.* Ithaca, NY: Cornell UP, 1984.

Bérubé, Michael, and Cary Nelson, eds. *Higher Education Under Fire: Politics, Economics and the Crisis of the Humanities.* New York: Routledge, 1995.

Bloom, Harold. *How to Read and Why.* New York: Scribner, 2000.

Bogart, Dave, ed. *Bowker Annual: Library and Book Trade Almanac, Facts, Figures and Reports*, New Providence, NJ: RR Bowker, vols from 1996–2002.

Booth, Wayne. *A Rhetoric of Fiction*, 2nd ed. Chicago: U of Chicago P, 1983.

——— *The Company We Keep.* Los Angeles: U of CA P, 1990.

Bourdieu, Pierre. *Distinction: A Social Critique of the Judgement of Taste.* Richard Nice, trans. Cambridge, MA: Harvard UP, 1984.

Brooks, David. *Bobos in Paradise: The New Upper Class and How They Got There.* New York: Simon and Schuster, 2000.

Brooks, Philip. *Oprah Winfrey: A Voice for the People.* New York: Grolier, 1999.

Chin, Paula, and Christina Cheakalos. "Touched by an Oprah." *People Magazine* 52:24 (December 20, 1999) 112–122.

Cloud, Dana L. "Hegemony or Concordance? The Rhetoric of Tokenism in 'Oprah' Winfrey's Rags-to-Riches Biography." *Critical Studies in Mass Communications* 13 (1996) 115–137.

Corcoran, Monica. "On the Dust Jacket: To O or Not to O." *New York Times* (October 21, 2001) 6+.

Davidson, Cathy N., ed. *Reading in America: Literary and Social History.* Baltimore: Johns Hopkins UP, 1989.

———— *Revolution and the Word: The Rise of the Novel in America.* New York: Oxford, 1986.

Devlin-Glass, Frances. "More Than a Reader and Less than a Critic: Literary Authority and Women's Book-Discussion Group" *Women's Studies International Forum* 24:5 (2001) 571–585.

Elliott, Jane. "O is for the Other Things She Gave Me: Franzen's *The Corrections* and contemporary women's fiction." *Bitch: Feminist Response to Pop Culture* 16 (Spring 2002) 70–74.

Epstein, Debbie and Deborah Lynn Steinberg. "All Het Up!: Rescuing Heterosexuality on the Oprah Winfrey Show." *Feminist Review* 54 (1996) 88–115.

———— "American Dreamin': Discoursing Liberally on the Oprah Winfrey Show." *Women's Studies International Forum* 21:1 (1998) 77–94.

Evans, Sara M., and Harry C. Boyte. *Free Spaces: The Sources of Democratic Change in America.* New York: Harper, 1986.

Ferguson, Roderick A. "Commodification, Difference and Discipline: Oprah's Book Club and African-American Literature." Author's unpublished manuscript, used with permission.

Flynn, Elizabeth A. and Patricinio P. Schweickart, eds. *Gender and Reading: Essays on Readers, Texts, and Contexts.* Baltimore: Johns Hopkins UP, 1986.

Franzen, Jonathan. "Meet Me in St. Louis." *The New Yorker* (December 18, 2001) newyorker.com posted December 17, 2001.

———— "Perchance to Dream: In the Age of Images, A Reason to Write Novels." *Harper's Magazine* 292:1751 (April 1996) 35+.

Gates, Henry Louis Jr. *The Signifying Monkey.* New York: Oxford, 1988.

Gere, Ann Ruggles. *Intimate Practices: Literacy and Cultural Work in U.S. Women's Clubs, 1880–1920.* Urbana: U of Illinois P, 1997.

Gladwell, Malcolm. "The Coolhunt" in *The Consumer Society Reader.* Juliet B. Schor and Douglas B. Holt, eds. New York: New Press, 2000. 360–374

Goldstein, Bill. "Let Us Now Praise Books Well Sold, Well Love, But Seldom Read." *New York Times,* (July 15, 2000) B11.

Guillory, John. *Cultural Capital: The Problem of Literary Canon Formation.* Chicago: U of Chicago P, 1993.

Haag, Laurie L. "Oprah Winfrey: The Construction of Intimacy in a Talk Show Setting." *Journal of Popular Culture* 26:4 (Spring 1993) 115–121.

Holt, Douglas B. "Does Cultural Capital Structure American Consumption?" in *The Consumer Society Reader.* Juliet B. Schor and Douglas B. Holt, eds. New York: New Press, 2000. 212–252.

Humble, Nicola. *The Feminine Middlebrow Novel 1920s to 1950s: Class, Domesticity, Bohemianism.* Oxford: Oxford UP, 2001.

Husni, Samir. qtd. in "Oprah Coast to Coast: A Phenomenon Struts Her Stuff on the Newsstand" by Alex Kuczynski. *New York Times* (October 2, 2000) C1.

Hutcheon, Linda. *A Poetics of Postmodernism: History, Theory, Ficton.* New York: Routledge, 1988.

Johnson, Marilyn and Dana Fineman. "Oprah Winfrey: A Life in Books." *Life* (September 1997) 44+.

Kacandes, Irene. *Talk Fiction: Literature and the Talk Explosion.* Lincoln: U of Nebraska P, 2001.

Kett, Joseph P. *The Pursuit of Knowledge Under Difficulties: From Self-Improvement to Adult Education in America, 1750–1990.* Stanford, CA: Stanford UP, 1994.

Kirkpatrick, David. "'Oprah' Gaffe by Franzen Draws Ire and Sales." *New York Times* (October 29, 2001) E1+.

————— "Winfrey Rescinds Offer to Author for Guest Appearance." *New York Times* (October 24, 2001) C4.

Korda, Michael. *Making the List: A Cultural History of the American Bestseller 1900–1999.* New York: Barnes and Noble, 2001.

Kuczynski, Alex. "Oprah Coast to Coast: A Phenomenon Struts Her Stuff on the Newsstand." *New York Times* (October 2, 2000) C1.

Lauter, Paul, ed. *Reconstructing American Literature: Courses, Syllabi, Issues.* Old Westbury, NY: Feminist P, 1983.

Long, Elizabeth. *The American Dream and the Popular Novel.* Boston: Routledge, 1985.

————— "The Book as Mass Commodity: The Audience Perspective." *Book Research Quarterly* (Spring 1987) 9–30.

————— *Book Clubs: Women and the Uses of Reading in Everyday Life.* Chicago: U of Chicago P, 2003.

—————"Reading Groups and the Postmodern Crisis of Cultural Authority." *Cultural Studies* 1:3 (October 1987) 306–327.

————— "Textual Interpretation as Collective Action." *Discourse* 14:3 (Summer 1992) 104–130.

————— "Women Reading Together: Book Groups, Subjectivity, and Social Change." Author's draft.

—————. "Women, Reading, and Cultural Authority: Some Implications of the Audience Perspective in Cultural Studies." *American Quarterly* 38:4 (Fall 1986) 591–612.

Lowe, Janet. *Oprah Winfrey Speaks: Insights from the World's Most Influential Voice.* New York: Wiley, 1998.

Lyotard, Jean-Francois. *The Postmodern Condition: A Report on Knowledge.* Minneapolis: U of Minnesota P, 1989.

MacDonald, Dwight. "Masscult and Midcult I." *Partisan Review* (Spring 1960) 203–233.

————— "Masscult and Midcult II." *Partisan Review* (Fall 1960) 589–631.

Maryles, Daisy (*Publishers Weekly* Executive Editor). "Bestsellers of 1996" in *Bowker Annual: Library and Book Trade Almanac, Facts, Figures and Reports,*

Dave Bogart, ed. New Providence, NJ: RR Bowker, 1997. 591–611. (Adapted from *Publishers Weekly*, April 7, 1997.)

———— "Bestsellers of 1997" in *Bowker Annual: Library and Book Trade Almanac, Facts, Figures and Reports*, Dave Bogart, ed. New Providence, NJ: RR Bowker, 1998. 610–621. (Adapted from *Publishers Weekly*, March 23, 1998.)

———— "Bestsellers of 1998" in *Bowker Annual: Library and Book Trade Almanac, Facts, Figures and Reports*, Dave Bogart, ed. New Providence, NJ: RR Bowker, 1999. 629–647. (Adapted from *Publishers Weekly*, March 29, 1999.)

———— "Bestsellers of 1999" in *Bowker Annual: Library and Book Trade Almanac, Facts, Figures and Reports*, Dave Bogart, ed. New Providence, NJ: RR Bowker, 2000. 625–644. (Adapted from *Publishers Weekly*, April 10, 2000.)

———— "Bestsellers of 2000" in *Bowker Annual: Library and Book Trade Almanac, Facts, Figures and Reports*, Dave Bogart, ed. New Providence, NJ: RR Bowker, 2001. 618–655. (Adapted from *Publisher Weekly*, March 19, 2001.)

———— "Bestsellers of 2001" in *Bowker Annual: Library and Book Trade Almanac, Facts, Figures and Reports*, Dave Bogart, ed. New Providence, NJ: RR Bowker, 2002. 659–677. (Adapted from *Publisher Weekly*, March 18, 2002.)

———— "Bestsellers of 2002" in *Bowker Annual: Library and Book Trade Almanac, Facts, Figures and Reports*, Dave Bogart, ed. New Providence, NJ: RR Bowker, 2003. 578–596. (Adapted from *Publisher Weekly*, March 24, 2003.)

Masciarotte, Gloria-Jean. "C'mon Girl: Oprah Winfrey and the Discourse of Feminine Talk." *Genders* 11 (Fall 1991) 81–110.

Max, D. T. "The Oprah Effect." *New York Times Magazine* (December 26, 1999) 36–41.

McCormick, Patrick. "Oprah Throws the Book at Us." *U.S. Catholic* (February 1997) 38–40.

McKinley, William, and Kattana Conley. "Literary Retailing and the (Re)Making of Popular Reading." *Journal of Popular Culture* 35:2 (Fall 2001) 207–221.

McNett, Gavin. "Reaching to the Converted." *Salon*, November 12, 1999. salon.com

Nelson, Dana D. "The Word in Black and White: Ideologies of Race and Literacy in Antebellum America" in *Reading in America: Literary and Social History*. Cathy N. Davidson, ed. Baltimore: Johns Hopkins UP, 1989. 140–156.

Nussbaum, Martha C. *Cultivating Humanity: A Classical Defense of Reform in Liberal Education*. Cambridge, MA: Harvard UP, 1997.

Ohmann, Richard. *Selling Culture: Magazines, Markets and Class at the Turn of the Century*. London: Verso, 1996.

———— "The Shaping of a Canon: U.S. Fiction, 1960–1975." *Critical Inquiry* 10:1 (September 1983) 199–22.

Peck, Janice. "Talk About Racism: Framing a Popular Discourse of Race on *Oprah Winfrey*." *Cultural Critique* 27 (Spring 1994) 89–126.

Popcorn, Faith, and Lys Marigold. *EVEolution: The Eight Truths of Marketing to Women*. New York: Hyperion, 2000.

Powell, Joanna. "I Was Trying to Fill Something Deeper." *Good Housekeeping* (October 1996).

Radway, Janice A. *A Feeling for Books: The Book-of-the-Month Club, Literary Taste, and Middle-Class Desire*. Chapel Hill: U of North Carolina P, 1997.

———— "The Scandal of the Middlebrow: The Book-of-the-Month Club, Class Fracture, and Cultural Authority." *South Atlantic Quarterly* 89:4 (Fall 1990) 703–736.

Richter, David H., ed. *The Critical Tradition: Classic Texts and Contemporary Trends*, 2nd ed. Boston: Bedford, 1998.

———— *Falling Into Theory: Conflicting Views on Reading Literature*, 2nd ed. Boston: Bedford, 1999.

Rooney, Kathy. "Oprah Learns Her Lesson." *The Nation* 274:19 (May 20, 2002) 56+.

Rubin, Joan Shelley. *The Making of Middlebrow Culture*. Chapel Hill: U of North Carolina P, 1992.

———— "Self, Culture, and Self-Culture in Modern America: The Early History of the Book-of-the-Month Club." *Journal of American History* 72:4 (March 1985) 782–806.

Scanlon, Jennifer, ed. *The Gender and Consumer Culture Reader*. New York: New York U P, 2000.

Schlosser, Eric. *Fast Food Nation: The Dark Side of the All-American Meal*. New York: HarperCollins, 2002.

Schor, Juliet B., and Douglas B. Holt, eds. *The Consumer Society Reader*. New York: New Press, 2000.

Schweickart, Patricinio P. "Reading Ourselves: Toward a Feminist Theory of Reading" in *Gender and Reading: Essays on Readers, Texts, and Contexts*. Elizabeth A. Flynn and Patricinio P. Schweickart, eds. Baltimore: Johns Hopkins UP, 1986. 31–62.

Sellers, Patricia. "The Business of Being Oprah." *Fortune* 145:7 (April 1, 2002) 50+.

Showalter, Elaine. *The New Feminist Criticism: Women, Literature, Theory*. New York: Pantheon, 1985.

Shulevitz, Judith. "You Read Your Book and I'll Read Mine." *New York Times Book Review* (May 19, 2002) 51.

Slezak, Ellen. *The Book Group Book: A Thoughtful Guide to Forming and Enjoying a Stimulating Book Discussion Group*, 3rd ed. Chicago: Chicago Review P, 2000.

Smith, Barbara Herrnstein. *Contingencies of Value: Alternative Perspectives for Critical Theory*. Cambridge, MA: Harvard UP, 1988.

Snyder, Gabriel. "When Oprah Stomped on Franzen, It Revealed a Vast Culture Split." *New York Observer* (November 1, 2001) 1+. nyoberver.com

Squire, Corinne. "Empowering Women? The Oprah Winfrey Show" in *Feminist Television Criticism: A Reader*, Charlotte Brunsdon, ed. New York: Oxford, 1997. 99–113.

Steiner, Wendy. "Look Who's Modern Now." *New York Times Book Review* (October 10, 1999) 7+.

Steyn, Mark. "Comic Oprah: America's Talker-in-Chief Is the Perfect Embodiment of the Virtual Culture of the Nineties." *National Review* 50:5 (March 23, 1998) 30+.

Tompkins, Jane. *Sensational Designs: The Cultural Work of American Fiction, 1790–1860*. New York: Oxford UP, 1985.

———— "Sentimental Power: *Uncle Tom's Cabin* and the Politics of Literary History" in *The New Feminist Criticism: Women, Literature, Theory*, Elaine Showalter, ed. New York: Pantheon, 1985. 81–104.

Weber, Bruce. "When the I's of a Novel Cross Over" *New York Times* (February 6, 1999), B7.

Williams, Mary Elizabeth. "Silence the Snobs!" *Salon*, November 12, 1999. salon.com

Williams, Raymond. *Marxism and Literature*. New York: Oxford UP, 1985.

Wolfe, Alan. *Moral Freedom: The Search for Virtue in a World of Choice*. New York: Norton, 2001.

Zeitchik, Steven, ed. *PW Newsline* (the daily newsmagazine of *Publishers Weekly* at publishersweekly.com) Various reports 2000–2003, including "Oprah's Biggest Successes" April 8, 2002 and "More Oprah: '99 was Host's Big Year" April 9, 2002.

Index

Adler, Mortimer, 85-88, 90, 96, 102, 107, 143n29
aesthetic authority, 96, 107
aesthetic choices, 78, 86, 87, 94, 101, 103–104
aesthetic freedom. *See* cultural democracy
aesthetic merit, 32, 62–63, 78, 80, 82–84, 103–104, 106. *See under* literary merit, standards of
aesthetic theory, 104, 107
African-American: heritage, 30, 68, 129n15; literary traditions (also Anglo-African), 30–32, 121–122n3, 127n7; writers, 21–22, 36
Ahab, 84, 88, 142n26
Alcott, Louisa May: *Little Women*, 42; *Rose in Bloom*, 37
Alger, Horatio, 33, 64. *See also* rags-to-riches
Allende, Isabelle, 14, 18, 23
American dream, 65, 72, 138–139n39
American century, 99, 146n1
American culture, 9, 24, 42, 53, 55, 68, 70, 80, 83, 94

American history: and self-improvement 32; and women, 25, 55–57
Angelou, Maya, 13, 18, 22, 70; *Heart of a Woman*, 13; *I Know Why the Caged Bird Sings*, 32
anticipatory marketing, 95
aristocracy, cultural, 83, 102, 107
Atwood, Margaret, 56
Austen, Jane, 1, 8, 37, 84–85, 96; *Emma*, 84–85; *Northanger Abbey*, 37

Back Roads (O'Dell), 27
Barnes and Noble, 5, 8
Baym, Nina, 38, 126n27
Bellow, Saul, 15
Beloved (Morrison), 30
Berg, Elizabeth, 18, 19, 63–64
bestseller, 2–3, 14–17, 20–22, 24, 78, 79, 82–83. *See also New York Times* bestseller lists
Binchy, Maeve, 18, 79
Black and Blue (Quindlen), 10, 13, 17, 61–63, 67
Bloom, Harold, 54, 77, 84–85, 87, 88, 90, 96, 107
Bobos in Paradise (Brooks), 100

Bluest Eye, The (Morrison), 14–15, 32, 63, 67–71, 89, 10
Bohjalian, Chris, 18
BOMC. *See* Book-of-the-Month Club
book club movement, 5, 42, 55, 56, 58, 67, 93, 95–97, 103
Book Group Book (Slezak), 55, 58–59
book groups: and aesthetic standards, 58–59, 84, 103–104, 107; and community, 57–58; and gender, 55; and social reading, 35, 54, 102; author's, 3, 59, 102; post-Oprah TV, 14, 72, 138n37; preoccupations of, 54, 66; proliferation of, 56, 66, 93, 95–97, 103, 134n4
Book of Ruth (Hamilton), 13, 39
Book-of-the-Month Club, 33–34, 82, 83–84, 123n8
Borders Bookstore, 8, 123n1
Bourdieu, Pierre, 86, 104
Brooks, David, 100–102
Breath, Eyes, Memory (Danticat), 13, 22

Cane River (Tademy), 20, 22, 65
celebrity, 3, 5, 29, 35, 53, 65, 70, 72, 77
Clark, Breena, 22
Cleage, Pearl, 22
College of St. Catherine, 2, 8, 19, 75, 88, 101
Color Purple, the (Walker), 21, 32
conversation: about aesthetic standards, 103–105; about books, 8, 11, 13, 41, 54, 88, 91, 96; with books, 41, 49, 54, 59; with other readers, 4, 49, 57, 59, 96, 103–104, 133n36

"Coolhunt, The," 95
Corcoran, Monica, 76
Corrections, The (Franzen), 4, 13, 75–78, 80, 88, 96; as Oprah's Book Club selection, 75–77; as Great American Novel, 75, 140n5
Cosby, Bill, 18, 22, 23
Couric, Katie, 30, 35, 138n37
critical reading, 40, 41, 45–50
cultural authority, 84
cultural capital, 78–88
cultural criticism, 78, 89, 96, 107
cultural democracy, 99, 101–108
cultural practices, 86
"cultural work," 62
culture wars, 5, 24, 107–108, 136–137n28, 146n50

Danticat, Edwidge, 13, 22, 79, 89, 94
Daughter of Fortune (Allende), 14, 18, 65
Davidson, Cathy, 33, 36–38, 129n14
Deep End of the Ocean (Mitchard), 11–12, 17, 39, 41–43, 89, 105
democracy, 4, 5, 36, 90, 101, 107; and literacy 33, 38; and novels, 36–38, 92. *See also* cultural democracy
democratic reading, 76, 87, 96, 103
democratic values, 27, 79, 92, 94, 97, 99–101
Devlin-Glass, Frances, 58
Dickey, Eric Jerome, 21
discussability, 104
Donohue, Phil, 96, 127n3, 145n46
Drowning Ruth (Schwarz), 50
Dr. Phil (Phil McGraw), 21, 65, 140–141n13
Dubus, Andre III, 13

East of Eden (Steinbeck), 2, 13, 17

economic capital, 78, 80; and cultural capital, 80–81, 83, 87–88

educate and entertain, to, 14, 37, 40. *See also* enlighten and entertain

Eliot, T.S., 35, 56, 102, 131n22, 135n9

Ellen Foster (Gibbons), 40, 65

Emma (Austen), 84–85

empathic reading, 41–42, 43, 47, 49–50, 61, 67, 69, 70, 72, 89, 102, 133n36

"emperor's new book," the, 23

enlighten and entertain, to, 9, 12, 14, 72, 102. *See also* educate and entertain

EVEolution: The Eight Truths of Marketing to Women (Popcorn), 95

Fall on Your Knees (MacDonald), 13, 65

Feeling for Books, A, (Radway), 83

feminist literary criticism, 5, 23, 24, 82, 85, 126nn25, 27, 133n36

Fine Balance, A, (Mistry), 13, 65

Fitch, Janet, 14, 106

Flynn, Elizabeth, 133n36

Franzen, Jonathan, 4, 13, 16, 75–77, 79, 88–89, 94, 96–97

Gaines, Ernest, 13, 22, 67

Gates, Henry Louis, Jr., 31, 121–122n3

Gatsby, Jay (*The Great Gatsby*), 78, 142n26

general reader, 49, 89, 93, 96, 143n29

Geraldo (Geraldo Rivera), 9

Gere, Ann Ruggles, 57

Gibbons, Kaye, 18–19, 40

Gladwell, Malcolm, 95

Gone With the Wind (Mitchell), 56

Good Life, the, 10, 40; and food, 81

Great Books, 35, 86, 89–90, 122n5

Grey, Zane, 8, 34

Gronniosaw, James Albert Ukawsaw, 31

Hamilton, Jane, 13, 18, 19, 67, 70, 94

Harper's magazine, 37, 75, 80, 96

Harpo, 20

Harris, E. Lynn, 21

Harry Potter and the Sorcerer's Stone (Rowley), 15

Haynes, Melinda, 19

Heart of a Woman (Angelou), 13, 18, 65, 70

Hedges, Elaine, 32

Hegi, Ursula, 14

Here on Earth (Hoffman), 13, 40

highbrow, 34, 35, 39, 50, 82

high culture, 4, 35, 53, 76–77, 79, 81, 87–88, 94, 97, 103, 141–142n17; accessibility of (through reading), 81–82; and low culture, 4, 35; and women, 35, 130–131n19; myth of, 24

Hoffman, Alice, 18

Holt, Douglas B., 87–88

House of Sand and Fog (Dubus), 13, 50, 65

How to Read a Book: A Classic Guide to Intelligent Reading (Adler and Van Doren), 85–88, 102, 107

How to Read and Why (Bloom), 54, 84, 90–91, 107

Humble, Nicola, 130–131n19

Husni, Samir, 26

I Know This Much is True (Lamb), 14
I Know Why the Caged Bird Sings
   (Angelou), 32
Icy Sparks (Rubio), 20
illiteracy, 10
improvement societies, 56–57
inspirational reading, 49–50, 69, 70,
   102
Intimate Practices: Literacy and Cultural
   Work in U.S. Women's Clubs,
   1880–1920 (Gere), 57

Jewel (Lott), 17, 27, 65
Joyce, James, 84

Kacandes, Irene, 121–122n, 145n46
King, Gayle, 46–47
King, Stephen, 3, 10, 21
Kingsolver, Barbara, 7, 14, 18, 42;
   Animal Dreams, 42; *Poisonwood*
   Bible, 14, 18, 63
Korda, Michael, 82

Lake, Ricki, 9
Lamb, Wally, 16, 18, 19, 67, 70; *She's*
   Come Undone, 10, 16, 39, 65, 66,
   89; *I Know This Much is True*, 14,
   16;
Lampher, Katherine, 55, 134n7
Lesson Before Dying, A (Gaines), 13, 22,
   65
Life magazine, 14
literacy, 29–30, 38, 56, 58, 80, 90,
   97: and African Americans,
   29–30, 127–128n7; and democracy, 33; and immigration,
   33–34, 38; and women, 37–38;
   cultural, 34, 91

literary criticism, 5, 8, 24, 50, 54,
   102, 136–137n28; traditional
   academic modes, 46–48, 50, 62,
   89
literary merit, standards of, 24, 84,
   86, 88–89, 92–94, 102–3,
   105–107
literary fiction, 3, 13–14, 34–35, 37,
   45, 76, 85–86
literary historians, 24, 33, 38, 50, 56.
   See also literary scholars
literary prizewinners, 14, 78, 93,
   124n10
literary salon, 10
literary scholars, 3, 15, 26, 83, 92,
   102
literary tradition: African-American,
   30–32; high art, 76–77, 78; traditional Western, 32, 80, 87
literary values, 96–97, 103
literature: American, 15, 35, 82, 92;
   classes, 13, 14, 24, 41, 45, 49,
   82, 85, 93, 102; classic, 8, 58,
   83; function of, 14, 54–55, 58,
   60, 62–63, 67, 69, 97, 108; serious, 2, 7, 12, 16, 24–25, 33, 36,
   76, 93, 94. 103; Western, 32
Little Bill books. *See* Cosby, Bill
Long, Elizabeth, Foreword ix–xii, 42,
   54, 56–57, 103, 132–133n35,
   147n10
lowbrow, 34, 39, 64, 82; and genre
   fiction, 35

MacDonald, Anne Marie, 13
Making the List, A Cultural History of the
   American Bestseller 1900–1999
   (Korda), 82–83

Map of the World (Hamilton), 13

Marxist literary criticism, 24

Maryles, Daisy, 3, 18, 19, 21

mass culture, 8, 75, 88, 90, 97. *See also*
   popular culture

mass marketing, 8, 21, 34, 38, 53, 75,
   84, 88, 97

Max, D.T., 20, 26, 64, 79, 81

McDonald, Dwight, 130–131n19,
   141–142n17

McDonald's, 82, 93

McGraw, Phil. *See* Dr. Phil

McHenry, Elizabeth, 127–128n7

McMillan, Terry, 21–22: *A Day Late
   and a Dollar Short*, 21; *How Stella
   Got her Groove Back*, 21; *Waiting to
   Exhale*, 21

McNett, Gavin, 26

Melville, Herman, 36, 82, 84

middlebrow, 34–36, 38, 40, 63, 72,
   130–131n19, 141–142n17: and
   the novel, 34–38, 63, 78, 81, 82,
   108, 130–131n19; book club,
   38–41, 56; reading, 50; vs. highbrow, 24–25, 103

Midwives (Bohjalian), 13, 17, 18, 65,
   96

Miller, Sue, 18, 63

Mistry, Rohinton, 13

Mitchard, Jacquelyn, 9, 11, 18, 19,
   41–43

MLA. *See* Modern Language Association

Modern Language Association, 25

Moral Freedom (Wolfe), 100

Morrison, Toni, 1, 12–13, 21–22, 26,
   30, 31, 38–40, 43–44, 45–48,
   67, 71, 82, 92, 94, 105: *Beloved*,

30; *Bluest Eye*, 14–15, 32, 63,
   67–71, 89, 103; *Paradise*, 13,
   15–16, 40, 45–49, 59, 67, 69,
   103; *Song of Solomon*, 1, 12–15,
   38–41, 43–45, 46, 49–50, 61,
   67; *Sula*, 65; and reading revolution, 1, 5, 26, 27, 104; and talking life, 1, 2, 51, 59–64, 66, 67,
   72, 92, 104, 121–122n3; as literary mentor, 13, 38–40, 45–51,
   67–71; on mothering, 69; on
   reading, 1, 13, 31, 40, 44–45,
   47–48, 94, 105; on virtues
   69–70; reading of, 40–41,
   45–51, 82

Mother of Pearl (Haynes), 20, 65

National Book Award, 15, 75,
   124n10

National Public Radio, 76, 87

Neidorf, Robin, 55, 58

Nelson, Dana D., 129n15

New York Times, 2, 75, 76: bestseller
   lists, 2–3, 10, 12, 15–19, 22,
   122n4; *Book Review*, 54, 83, 92,
   122n4; *Magazine*, 20, 26, 64, 79

Nobel Prize (for literature), 15, 69

Northanger Abbey (Austen), 37

novel-reading: American tradition of,
   56; as foundation for democracy, 37–38, 83; in conduct
   books and sermons, 37

novels: academic responses to,
   13–14, 42, 62, 78, 80; and class
   distinctions, 36–38, 82; and
   classical texts, 36, 82; and com-
   mercialism, 24, 77, 80, 86; and
   gender, 23–25, 36–38, 92–93;

novels (*continued*): and genre, 35, 37;
and materialism, 34; and social
issues, 30, 32, 43, 61–64, 67, 82,
87, 102; and social justice, 32,
66, 102; as educational tools,
36–38, 40; as therapy, 26; as
works of art, 13–14, 43, 63, 71,
72; commodification of, 78–80,
86; cowboy, 8, 24, 34; first,
9–10, 18–20; Great American,
75; literary, 3, 13–14, 34–35,
37, 45, 76, 85–86, 94, 97; middlebrow, 34–38, 39, 63, 78, 81,
82, 108, 130–131n19; mystery,
35; Oprah-type, 5, 13–14, 20,
23, 72, 77, 78, 89; sentimental,
82; social function of, 1–2, 4,
61–64, 71–72, 82, 87–88,
95–97, 102, 107; talking life of,
1, 2, 31, 59–64, 66, 67, 72–73,
92, 104, 121–122n3; teaching of
(in colleges), 82–83, 88–89; vs.
self-help books, 3–4, 21, 35
NPR. *See* National Public Radio
Nussbaum, Martha, 146n50

O magazine, 26
Oates, Joyce Carol, 7, 13, 67, 94
Open House (Berg), 13, 50, 63–64, 67,
89
Oprah. *See* Winfrey, Oprah
Oprah! (talk show), 29, 40, 45, 65,
67, 79–80, 101; and ratings,
77
Oprah effect, the, 14, 19
Oprahfication, 53–54, 60–63, 78,
133n1. *See also* oprahfy
oprahfy, 53, 72

Oprah's Book Club: access to readers,
14, 68, 72, 76, 94–96; and first
six years, 2, 20; and social reading, 45, 60, 67; as offshoot of
celebrity culture, 65, 72; as
women's club, 56; class (at College of St. Catherine), 3, 53,
88–89, 105–107; end of, 1,
122n5; first meeting, 8–9,
41–43; format of, 10–11; reading lessons of, 41, 43–51,
67–69, 71, 104; responses to 7,
25–26, 76, 80; return of, 2, 17;
success of, 1–5, 10, 27, 34, 77,
78, 80, 97; selecting books for,
20, 39, 144n43; setting of 10,
66, 68, 81; themes of, 65–66;
valuing readers in, 25, 72
Oprah seal, 4, 76–77, 80, 88
Oufkir, Malika, 23

Paradise (Morrison), 13, 40, 45–49,
59, 67, 69, 103
People magazine, 18, 35, 75
Pilot's Wife, The (Shreve), 13, 21, 65,
91, 94
poetry: as highbrow literature, 35,
131n22; as doggerel, 131n22
Poisonwood Bible (Kingsolver), 14, 18,
63
Popcorn, Faith, 95
popular culture, 8, 97, 107
postmodern, 92, 93, 101, 104, 147n6
Potter, Harry, 2
Princeton University, 13, 46
Publishers Weekly, 3, 9, 15, 18, 19,
21
Pulitzer Prize, 15